Guide to emotional health

1. Which two short questionnaires can pinpoint a drinking problem?

2. Can your morning coffee have a negative effect on your emotions?

3. Can fluorescent lights chase away the blues?

4. Name two diseases with genetic roots that are triggered by stress and fatigue.

5. Is fingernail biting just a bad habit?

6. Is there a 24-hour hotline for domestic abuse?

7. How many American women are raped at some time in their lives?

**ISN'T IT IMPORTANT THAT YOU HAVE THE FACTS? YOUR LIFE AND YOUR HEALTH MAY DEPEND ON IT.**

*Answers:*

1. *The CAGE and T-ACE questionnaires*
2. *Yes, caffeine can produce anxiety as well as interfere with sleep.*
3. *Special types are used to reduce symptoms of SAD (seasonal affective disorder).*
4. *Migraines and eczema*
5. *No, it is clearly related to psychological stress.*
6. *Yes, 202-232-6682*
7. *One in every eight*

The American Medical Women's Association

# Guide to Emotional Health

Medical Co-editors
**Roselyn Payne Epps, M.D., M.P.H.,
M.A., F.A.A.P.
Susan Cobb Stewart, M.D., F.A.C.P.**

A Dell Book

Published by
Dell Publishing
a division of
Bantam Doubleday Dell Publishing Group, Inc.
1540 Broadway
New York, New York 10036

This material was originally published along with other material in THE WOMEN'S COMPLETE HEALTHBOOK published by Delacorte Press.

Illustrations by Wendy Frost

ISBN: 0-440-22248-6

Reprinted by arrangement with Delacorte Press

Printed in the United States of America

Published simultaneously in Canada

September 1996

10 9 8 7 6 5 4 3 2 1

OPM

# The AMWA Guide to Emotional Health

Roselyn Payne Epps, M.D., M.P.H., M.A.,
and Susan Cobb Stewart, M.D.

A healthy mind is one of the most important components of general good health. Emotional fitness and social well-being are also essential for maintaining a sound mind and body. The American Medical Women's Association, the world's largest and most prestigious organization of women physicians and medical specialists, believes that women must avoid a disease-oriented approach to women's health and focus on maintaining optimal health on a daily and long-term basis. The more a woman knows about her mind and how it relates to her body and its functions, the better equipped she will be to safeguard good health through preventive strategies, such as sleeping properly and reducing stress. The content of *The AMWA Guide to Emotional Health* is divided into four sections:

Part I, Emotional Health, presents strategies for improving emotional and mental well-being. This section discusses in-depth many common mental conditions, such as eating and sleep disorders, as well as mood disorders and more severe mental illnesses. This section presents a range of mental health therapy options designed to help women better understand various approaches to treating and coping with such problems.

Part II, Staying Healthy in Spite of Stress, shows how emotional stress relates to the body as a whole, while presenting tips on how to relieve stress in everyday life. This section helps women identify both the psychological and the physical symptoms of stress. Also discussed in great detail are the reasons women are particularly vulnerable to the devastating effects of stress.

Part III, Violence and Women, shows that violent

crimes against women are being reported more frequently than ever in the 1990s. Rape, date rape, the aftermath of childhood sexual abuse, and domestic battery are all major areas of concern among women, who must be able to recognize the circumstances and effects of violence against them. For victims, this section counsels women on how to seek help—emotional, legal, or physical—and how to prevent abuse from occurring in the future.

Part IV, Substance Abuse in Women, thoroughly investigates drug and alcohol abuse among women. It presents the historical bases for substance abuse and identifies the harmful impact it can have on a woman's body, mind, and relationships. Ways to recognize and avoid substance abuse are cited and fully explained. For those who need help, this section advises practical self-help methods and gives listings for relevant national and community resources.

*The AMWA Guide to Emotional Health* provides authoritative information that all women need in today's changing environment. It illuminates emotional health concerns unique to women in the 1990s and offers sound medical advice. Supported by the expertise and experience of the American Medical Women's Association, *The AMWA Guide to Emotional Health* offers a sensitive and sensible approach to helping women live a mentally stable and emotionally healthy life.

# CONTENTS

**PART I:**
**EMOTIONAL HEALTH**
*Leah J. Dickstein, M.D., F.A.P.A.*

Strategies for Improving Your Emotional Health 3
Mental Health Specialists 7
Types of Therapies 8
Anxiety 9
Depression and Other Mood Disorders 16
Dissociative Disorders 25
Personality Disorders 27
Schizophrenia 32
Mental Disorders Due to a General
   Medical Condition 35
Sleep Disorders 36
Eating Disorders 41

**PART II:**
**STAYING HEALTHY IN SPITE OF STRESS**
*Jeanne Spurlock, M.D., F.A.P.A.*

How Stress Affects the Body 49
How to Cope with Stress 55
Listen to Your Body 62

**PART III:**
**VIOLENCE AND WOMEN**
*Marjorie Braude, M.D.*

A Growing Call for Action 67
The Effects of Violence on Women 69
Rape 70
Childhood Sexual Abuse 83
Domestic Battery 87

PART IV:
SUBSTANCE ABUSE IN WOMEN
*Roselyn Payne Epps, M.D., M.P.H, M.A., F.A.A.P.
and Anne Geller, M.D.*

How Drugs Affect the Mind and Body                99
Who Is at Risk?                                  102
Types of Drugs and Their Effects                 103
Impact of Smoking on Women                       107
Smoking and Reproduction                         111
How to Quit Smoking                              112
Alcohol                                          117
Alcohol and the Special Concerns of Women        122
When Drinking Becomes a Problem                  123
Prescription Drugs                               127
Illicit Drugs                                    130
Informed Avoidance of Substance Abuse            135
Editors and Contributors                         139
Index                                            141

The American Medical Women's Association

# Guide to Emotional Health

# PART I
# Emotional Health

Leah J. Dickstein, M.D., F.A.P.A.

Throughout the life cycle, the psychological development of women differs substantially from that of men. The modern woman must contend with a changing image and conflicting societal demands that impose varying degrees of stress on her mental and emotional resources. As a young woman, for example, she may find that an abnormal concern for the perfect body as depicted in the popular media may lead to a lifelong dissatisfaction with her own body and perhaps even to an eating disorder. In her twenties and thirties, as the stresses of work outside the home and family life merge, she may experience acute anxiety and exhaustion as she attempts to do everything. In her forties and fifties, menopausal symptoms, the fear of growing older, and being part of the sandwich generation caring for elderly relatives as well as her young adult children and possibly grandchildren, in addition to her home and outside work, may trigger depression or the onset of anxiety.

Fortunately, most of these symptoms of mental upheaval do not affect the majority of American women, who seem to manage their emotional ups and downs successfully themselves. And, certainly, it is not necessary to seek the help of mental health professionals at every sign of mild, short-term episodes of anxiety or the "blues." Occasional moodiness or a depressed feeling is not likely to be symptomatic of mental disturbance, but merely a part of everyday functioning.

If you are trying to gain control over your emotions and your life, take advantage of the resources around you. It helps to sit down quietly and sort out the stresses in your life that are disturbing you. Don't blame others for your problems. Instead, take a good look at your responses to daily events and see how you can make adjustments that might make a substantial difference in your life. Cultivate some strategies that will help you get through your life with fewer complications and frustrations. Above all, after reviewing your issues, communicate clearly with the important people in your life.

# STRATEGIES FOR IMPROVING YOUR EMOTIONAL HEALTH

We know that to succeed in the world we must have inner discipline and a sense of control over our lives. This doesn't mean that we always accomplish what we set out to do or that we don't suffer disappointments and losses along the way. Here are some suggestions to prevent the stresses and strains of everyday life from adversely affecting your mental and emotional health:

- *Have a physical check-up.* Often what appears to be a mental disorder is actually the result of a physical problem. For example, if you are chronically tired and depressed, you may be suffering from a thyroid condition that is sapping your energy. If you are experiencing panic attacks—when your heart races and you break out in a sweat—you may have the symptoms of hypoglycemia. It's always best to rule out physical causes first.

- *Exercise regularly.* Your physical well-being is the basic foundation of your mental and emotional well-being. Daily vigorous exercise helps lower the level of triglycerides in the blood and stimulates the production of endorphins, a morphine-like chemical that helps to counteract feelings of anxiety and depression. Many women also find that exercise can help alleviate the symptoms of premenstrual syndrome (PMS), perhaps because PMS has been proven to create sudden drops in the levels of endorphins released in the brain. Regular exercise also will help you be more relaxed during the day and sleep better at night. Before beginning an exercise program you should have a complete physical examination.

■ *Eat the right foods.* A nutritious diet—with lots of fruit, vegetables, and whole grains and low-fat meats and fish—is essential to good health. But it's also important to avoid foods that have a strong effect on your moods and can disrupt the body's smooth functioning. Caffeine in coffee, tea, and soft drinks, for example, is a stimulant that produces anxiety and interferes with sleep and many medications in many people. Caffeine stimulates the locus coeruleus, which is located in the medulla oblongata, the site in the brain that is responsible for "fight or flight," a primitive human reaction to any sign of danger, real or imagined.

Sugar is another culprit. You may crave sugar at certain times of the day because your blood sugar is low. But eating sugar on a daily basis just increases your blood sugar highs and lows. If you cut sugar out of your diet, you will find that you no longer have the urge for it; your energy level and your mood will also remain constant throughout the day. Women with PMS tend to crave sugar, but studies have shown that women who remove sugar from their diets experience fewer PMS symptoms, including less anxiety and depression. And, of course, avoid smoking, drugs, and the excessive use of alcohol.

■ *Take control of your life.* It is our attitudes and response to the events and vicissitudes of life that determine our life story. Use your losses as a means of enriching your life experience and as a learning opportunity. Review your lifestyle choices and their effect on your well-being. Sometimes changing some aspect of your life, although difficult, may be the best path toward a positive mental outlook. If you hate your job, for example, seek out another one—remaining in a demeaning situation will only make your anxiety and depression worse. Be cautious, however. Although moving, changing jobs, and leaving destructive relationships all have the potential to change your state of mind for the better, it is not always a solution. If you do not clearly identify the source of your problems, you may find yourself in a new job or in a new relationship with all the same anxieties and frustrations. As the old adage says, "You can change your skies, but not yourself." It is absolutely essential that you try and understand the specific sources of your distress before you make radical changes in your life, especially if others will be adversely affected, such as children or other loved ones.

- *Keep busy, but not too busy.* Certainly one of the best ways to avoid depression is to keep active. Many women find that when they are engrossed in their work, they tend to be happier. It is important to work, plan for the future, and set goals, but it's vital to enjoy life's pleasures, too. Use your leisure time for a hobby or acquiring a new skill, and take the time to relax. Relaxation—whether through yoga, meditation, relaxation tapes, or biofeedback—is another tool you have to control your state of mind. After practicing a method for a few weeks, you will more than likely be able to lower your anxiety level.

- *Become socially involved.* A balanced life is one that incorporates personal and social activities equally. Friends, especially, can help in times of mental or physical distress. If you can relieve your tensions by talking to a friend who experienced a similar situation, you may find that you are not alone and that you are more normal than you think. Trying to figure out all of your problems alone may be a fruitless task because in isolation you can lose perspective.

If you experience increasing anxiety and depression, whether realistic or irrational, you may gain some insight and help from a good self-help book or from interaction with a self-help group. Sometimes, however, our problems are too overwhelming or severe for the more simple solutions. When that happens, you will need the advice and counsel of a competent mental health professional.

# MENTAL HEALTH SPECIALISTS

Several kinds of professionals, with different types of training, can provide treatment for a wide range of mental and emotional needs. *Psychiatrists* are licensed physicians who specialize in the mental health field. They are the only mental health professionals who can take a complete medical history and understand the interactions of physical illness with emotions, and prescribe drugs. Their form of psychiatric treatment often combines drug therapy with psychotherapy. *Psychologists* have academic doctoral degrees in the field of psychology. They are not medical doctors, however, and cannot prescribe medication. Psychologists often use psychotherapy in treating their patients and refer patients to psychiatrists if and when they believe psychotherapy alone is not the correct treatment. *Psychiatric social workers* have academic degrees in the field of social work with advanced training in psychotherapy. Many of these practitioners are excellent counselors, but they do not have the depth of psychological training that psychologists do.

When you consult a professional, don't be afraid to ask as many questions as you wish. Remember, a consultation is not a commitment. The practitioner should help you understand your problem and should make a number of suggestions as to the alternative therapies available. A preliminary consultation will also give you a sense of what it would be like to work with that particular person.

## TYPES OF THERAPIES

Psychotherapy—also called "one on one"—takes place between you and your therapist. Its goal is to make you feel better as you share your personal life experiences with the therapist and gain insight and understanding into your behavior and emotions. There are a number of different types of psychotherapy.

*Psychoanalysis* is an intensive form of psychotherapy that enables you to explore your conscious and unconscious thoughts, as well as your childhood conflicts and early relationships. Psychoanalysis is usually a long-term therapy that takes several years to complete. *Cognitive therapy* can help you to correct negative thinking patterns and explore how you view yourself in your environment. This type of therapy is short term, usually requiring a maximum of 10 to 12 visits. *Behavioral therapy* is based on the principles of operant conditioning, the reinforcement of behavior by reward and punishment. Psychotherapists engaged in behavior modification use various techniques to retrain your impulses and mode of thinking, including systematic desensitization and counterconditioning. *Marriage and family or dyadic therapy* attempts to resolve conflicts within the family setting. Members of the family come to the therapist either singly or together and talk openly about the problems experienced within the marriage and/or family or relationship structure. Usually short term, this type of counseling attempts to find reasonable alternatives and solutions to destructive family and relationship dynamics. *Group therapy* is also a very useful form of therapy. All of these therapies, or variations of them, are used to treat anxiety, depression, phobias, and other mental and emotional disorders.

# ANXIETY

Anxiety is a vague kind of fear or tension that occurs when you sense something unpleasant or threatening is about to happen. Some anxiety is a normal reaction in certain situations—a sense of anxiety may even improve performance—but persistent, irrational anxiety can cause physical symptoms such as rapid heartbeat, dry mouth, dizziness, intestinal problems, an inability to concentrate, irritability, insomnia, and even a fear of impending doom.

Anxiety can appear in several forms. Psychiatrists classify anxiety into the following types: generalized anxiety disorder, obsessive-compulsive disorder, panic disorder, simple phobias, and post-traumatic stress disorder.

## Generalized Anxiety Disorder (GAD)

This type of anxiety can spread throughout many areas in a person's life, creating a constant state of tension and worry called "free-floating" anxiety. GAD makes one feel as if something terrible is going to happen at any moment. This state of dread often causes a secondary anxiety that makes the sufferer worry that the anxiety itself will cause her to lose her job or develop an illness or even "lose her mind."

GAD most commonly occurs in young adults, often following a period of major depression. The physical symptoms can include palpitations, diarrhea, chronic muscle tension, nervous twitches, breathing problems, headaches, sweaty hands, insomnia, and the general "jitters." In half the patients who experience an anxiety disorder, mild to moderate depression can also accompany the anxiety. A number of antidepressants have antianxiety features as well; thus one medication can alleviate depressive and anxiety symptoms.

*Treatment:* After a physical examination and a complete history is obtained to rule out any other medical disorder, a psychiatrist can prescribe the appropriate medication to relieve this anxiety and depression. You will also be encouraged to begin therapy. The treatment of anxiety disorders varies, but a combination of drugs and behavioral therapy seems to be most effective. Behavioral therapy focuses on the specific patterns of behavior that are distressing to the patient or interfering with daily functioning; psychoanalysis has been found overall to be less effective in these cases.

Psychiatrists treat anxiety disorders with a group of drugs called anxiolytics. These medications must be used with caution because of their addictive qualities. Most of these drugs are from the family of benzodiazepines, which includes alprazolam (Xanax) and diazepam (Valium). Usually taken in pill form, anxiolytics have potential side effects, including confusion, lethargy, and an inability to coordinate muscle movement. Clonazepam (Klonopin) and buspirone (BuSpar) are newer antianxiety agents. If you are taking any of these medications, don't drink alcohol or use caffeine, and watch your driving and other use of machines early in treatment. Never use over-the-counter medications without checking with your physician first. In some cases, the drug may cause you to develop new anxieties. If that happens, check with your physician; she or he will probably reduce or discontinue the drug treatment. It is also important to gradually decrease the dose of anxiolytics: if treatment is stopped abruptly, serious withdrawal effects can occur, including severe nightmares, insomnia, and seizures.

## Obsessive-Compulsive Disorder (OCD)

The symptoms of obsessive-compulsive disorder usually appear first during adolescence or early adulthood. The obsessive part of the disorder is characterized by an idea or impulse that recurs involuntarily, despite the attempt of the afflicted person to stop or suppress these thoughts and impulses. The compulsive behavior is demonstrated by a compelling urge to repeat a behavior or ritual to eliminate or counteract the obsession, even though that behavior appears to be senseless. For example, an individual may be obsessive-compulsive about cleanliness and wash her hands dozens of times during the day. Or she may check countless times to make sure she has completed a specific task, such as turning off the stove or locking the door.

OCD affects about 1 to 2 percent of the population. Anxiety disorders, like many other medical illnesses, entail a genetic predisposition; that is, they run in families. Those who suffer from the disorder tend to have rigid and orderly personalities. If they are not allowed to perform their daily rituals and obsessive actions, they usually become overwhelmed with anxiety and fear.

*Treatment:* As with generalized anxiety disorder, OCD usually responds to behavioral therapy. The idea is to gradually expose the OCD patient to the situation that provokes the undesirable behavior. In most cases, a combination of drug treatment and behavioral therapy can reduce or eliminate the obsessive-compulsive impulses and rituals. Specific antidepressants may be used to counteract the anxiety disorder as well as the accompanying depression.

# Panic Disorder

Panic disorder starts with a sudden feeling of intense dread, apprehension, and a sense of impending doom. Physical symptoms include heart palpitations, shortness of breath, dizziness, weakness, sweating, choking, nausea, and a numbness or tingling sensation in the extremities. The symptoms can be so severe that a sufferer may rush to the hospital thinking she is having a heart attack. In fact, because of its physiological symptoms, panic disorder is often misdiagnosed as a respiratory or cardiac problem.

People who suffer from panic disorder often link their attacks to the specific place where they occurred. For example, if they have an attack in a crowded elevator or in an airplane, they will avoid elevators and planes as possible triggers of further attacks. As a result, many sufferers severely limit their activities; some eventually develop a fear of going out of their homes at all, developing a phobia known as agoraphobia. Women in particular are more likely to suffer from panic disorder with agoraphobia.

Researchers have found that panic disorder, like generalized anxiety disorder, has a genetic component. It is thought that panic attacks originate in the locus coeruleus, which produces norepinephrine, a chemical used for the "fight or flight" response. Too much of this substance produces anxiety and fear. As people age, the locus coeruleus produces lower levels of the chemical, so older people tend to have fewer, if any, panic attack episodes.

*Treatment:* The medications commonly used to relieve panic attacks are either the tricyclic antidepressants or the selective serotonin reuptake inhibitors. Antianxiety drugs may also be effective to relieve the initial fear of the attacks themselves. Behavior modification combined with relaxation therapy can be a valuable alternative or complement to medication.

# Phobias

Among the most common anxiety disorders, simple phobias are characterized by a constant irrational fear of a particular object, activity, place, or situation. The phobic person may have a clear understanding of how senseless the phobia is but still have a persistent desire to avoid its cause. Many types of phobias exist, including:

- *Ailurophobia*—a fear of cats.
- *Belonephobia*—a fear of sharp objects.

- *Claustrophobia*—a fear of enclosed spaces.
- *Monophobia*—a fear of being alone.
- *Acrophobia*—a fear of heights.
- *Sitophobia*—a fear of food.
- *Pterygophobia*—a fear of flying.
- *Ocholophobia*—a fear of crowds.
- *Acaraphobia*—a fear of small insects.
- *Agoraphobia*—a fear of public or open spaces.

Although minor fears exist in everyone, a true phobia can alter a person's behavior and lifestyle. For example, if you live in the country and you are afraid of a city subway system, it's not a real problem because you can manage quite successfully without having to take a subway. But if you need to move to the city to take the job of your dreams, you may find that your fear of subways seriously restricts your life.

*Treatment:* Phobias can often be successfully treated with behavior modification therapy, using a technique called systematic desensitization. In desensitization therapy, you are repeatedly exposed to the anxiety-provoking stimulus while in a deep state of relaxation. During repeated visits to the therapist, you are led through a process of increasing exposure until your fear and anxiety gradually diminish. Many people require medication as well.

## Post-Traumatic Stress Disorder (PTSD)

If you have witnessed or experienced an intensely traumatic situation or event, you may later suffer from post-traumatic stress disorder (PTSD). This disorder is characterized by a chronic reexperiencing of the traumatic event in the form of nightmares, hallucinations, and recurring flashes of memory. You may suffer from insomnia, decreased sexual drive, heightened sensitivity to noise, depression, anxiety, and intense irritability. You may also feel isolated from other people and withdraw socially. Victims of PTSD can relive the stressful event for weeks, months, or years at a time while showing a numbness to their present surroundings.

Not surprisingly, most of the knowledge of PTSD comes from research conducted on veterans of World War II and the Korean and Vietnam conflicts. Survivors of rape and other crimes may also suffer from this condition. Although PTSD is classified as an anxiety disorder, it is a response to an actual experience and is therefore considered to be more of a normal reaction to an overwhelming trauma and shock. The severity of PTSD is directly linked to the psychological strength of the person before the event took place. Symptoms usually appear shortly after the trauma, but in some cases the disorder is not apparent until after an incubation period of several months. The symptoms typically disappear after about six months, but in some cases they can recur for years afterward.

*Treatment:* A psychiatrist can prescribe the appropriate medications to relieve your depression and anxiety. You will also be encouraged to begin therapy to talk out the problem and to formulate ways to control your thoughts and inner reactions.

# DEPRESSION AND OTHER MOOD DISORDERS

Depression is a common psychological condition that affects millions of Americans to varying degrees. It can occur without any apparent reason, although current research supports the belief that complex psychological, environmental, and biochemical changes may trigger the initial mood swing. Depression also may be an inherited condition.

Sadness, grief, and a depressed feeling are all normal reactions to a serious loss or tragic event. And everyone suffers now and again from a mild case of the "blues." Major depression, however, persists to the point where it interferes with your daily tasks, impairing your ability to live a normal life. In many cases, the cause of major depression is unknown. A sad or traumatic event is often the trigger. Some medications can bring on a bout of depression. A severe lowering of mood can even occur as a reaction to a lack of sunlight during the fall and winter months.

## Symptoms of Depression

Often it is difficult for physicians and patients to recognize a case of major depression. A true depression is characterized by the following signs and symptoms.

- *Negativity in all aspects of life.* You have a feeling of pessimism and the belief that nothing can make your life better.

- *Changes in sleep patterns.* Typically, there is ini-

tial insomnia or you wake up in the middle of
the night and can't get back to sleep again. Or
you have early morning awakening at 2:00,
3:00, or 4:00 A.M. Or you sleep more than is
necessary.

- *Change in eating patterns.* You have a lack of or
  change in appetite and eat either too little and
  lose weight, or too much and gain weight.

- *Fatigue.* You experience a lack of energy that
  permeates everything you do, including a
  declining interest in your work, leisure activities, and sex. You have difficulty concentrating
  or making decisions.

- *Isolation.* You feel anxious or uninterested in
  social situations and gradually withdraw from
  people. You may neglect your appearance.

- *Persistent sadness and self-loathing.* You develop
  a lack of self-confidence and feel a sense of
  worthlessness. You have frequent bouts of crying
  for no reason. Your feelings of hopelessness may
  lead to thoughts of and plans for suicide.

Studies have shown that individuals are more
prone to depression at certain times of life. Depression in women first may occur in adolescence when
the pressures of becoming a young woman in our
society, together with school and the issues of breaking away from the family and facing adulthood, often
cause teenagers to doubt themselves and turn inward.
Divorce, sexual problems, a limited work horizon,
personal disappointments, and past unresolved grief
and abuse issues may bring on depression in the middle years. Depression among the elderly is also com-

# WINTER BLUES

Although many people find the dark, dreary days of January and February to be depressing, there are some who suffer much more deeply at this time of the year. They experience what is called seasonal affective disorder (SAD). More women than men have this condition, which typically occurs in the winter months when sunlight is at a minimum.

During the colder part of the year, the pineal gland, located at the bottom of the brain, secretes a hormone called melatonin. This hormone is associated with drowsiness and lethargy. Although most people are not affected by the surplus of melatonin in their brains, SAD sufferers cannot tolerate the excess hormone and become severely depressed and debilitated. Researchers have found that light therapy—the use of specially designed fluorescent lights that mimic the sun's rays—can enable most of these people to recover their normal energy and emotional stability.

mon and may be attributable to the death of friends and family, physical and mental limitations, and thoughts of impending death. Women especially are liable to experiencing depression associated with hormonal changes in the body. Women experience depression twice as frequently as men.

# Hormonal Depression

Chemical depression, or hormonally induced depression is common among pregnant women and among those who suffer a spontaneous abortion or undergo a hysterectomy. Some women suffer from postpartum depression after childbirth. Women in their thirties and forties may experience premenstrual syndrome (PMS). Premenstrual dysphoric disorder (PMDD) is the feeling of tension, irritability, and depression that occurs every month for up to two weeks before menses. Although PMS is still poorly understood, it is thought to be the result of hormonal changes in the body and seriously affects approximately 5 percent of women.

*Treatment:* At least one out of five Americans will suffer from severe depression in their lives and only one of every five depressed adults will seek treatment. It is therefore important to realize the available options for treating this serious mental disorder. A common treatment includes both the use of antidepressant medications and psychotherapy.

Within 4 to 6 weeks after starting drug therapy, you should begin to feel the benefit of the prescribed antidepressant. (Many physicians are inclined to prescribe a low dosage, at first, with gradual increases to the therapeutic level.) Drug treatment for depression usually lasts between 6 months and a year. Recent research has shown that many people benefit from continuing the use of antidepressants after recovery, because it can help avoid another depressive episode. When the drug therapy is seen as no longer necessary, tapering off the dosage gradually is best or serious side effects may result. Typical medications used in the treatment of depression include the tricyclic antidepressants, monoamine oxidase inhibitors, selective serotonin reuptake inhibitors, and lithium. Tricyclic antidepressants, unlike amphetamines, do not raise your mood artificially, but simply relieve the depression. The type of tricyclic chosen depends upon which side effects you can handle most easily. Some of the drugs in the amitriptyline (Elavil) class will make you feel somewhat lethargic and thus may be a good choice if you are nervous or overanxious or have problems with insomnia. Common side effects of these antidepressants may include constipation, dry mouth, temporary blurred vision, minor urinary tract problems, and dizzy spells. Elderly people may suffer from short-term memory loss and temporary impotence. Antidepressants affect different people in varying ways, and each drug must be given an allotted amount of time before it is expected to take effect.

Other popular antidepressant treatments include the following:

■ *Fluoxetine (Prozac)*. One of the most useful of the new antidepressants on the market, Prozac (fluoxetine) takes effect in about three weeks and works with a standard dose level. Known side effects include anxiety, a decrease in appetite, headache, and nausea. Sertraline (Zoloft) and paroxetine (Paxil) are two other very effective SSRIs.

■ *Monoamine oxidase (MAO) inhibitors.* MAO inhibitors are used when the tricyclic or SSRI antidepressants don't work, especially for what is called atypical depression. These drugs are very effective and work quickly, but their side effects can be more dangerous than the tricyclics. One disadvantage is that MAO inhibitors react dangerously with a number of different foods, including aged cheese, red wine, pickled herring, and beer.

■ *Electroshock therapy (EST)*. Formerly thought to be dangerous, electroshock therapy is now considered a very safe and effective treatment for major depression. It is one of the fastest ways to get results and is also painless. EST is usually administered to severely depressed or suicidal patients in a hospital setting, but it can be used on an outpatient basis as well. Short-term memory loss is the major side effect of EST, but most disruptions of memory are resolved within 6 to 9 months after treatment. EST is usually followed by psychotherapy and antidepressant medication under a psychiatrist's care.

## Bipolar Disorder

Bipolar disorder, formerly called manic-depressive disorder, is a mental condition characterized by bouts of depression followed or preceded by manic exuberance and enthusiasm. The change in mood is often accompanied by irrational thoughts and periods of anger or rage. The manic phase includes irritability, grandiosity, and a sense of elation. The person is sleepless, talks a great deal, displays impulsive behavior, and often is irresponsible with money and goes on spending sprees. In some people the manic episodes are more frequent, while others experience more depression.

Bipolar disorder differs from major depression in a number of ways. It is much less common. It occurs with equal frequency among men and women, and they do not generally display the low self-esteem or obsessive thinking that those suffering from major depression do. Also, while major depression can occur at any time during the life cycle, bipolar disorder usually occurs before the age of thirty. Finally, bipolar disorder is characterized by frequent short outbursts, while major depression lasts longer and occurs less often. For all these reasons, researchers believe that major depression and bipolar disorder spring from different roots, although both have a genetic basis, that is, occur in other family members.

## Dysthymia and Cyclothymia

People who pass through phases of depression throughout their lives but otherwise function normally may have dysthymia or cyclothymia. These mild disorders are characterized by patterns of repetitive depression, but the patient may fail to display enough symptoms to be classified as suffering from major depression or from bipolar disorder. *Dysthymia* is a chronic mild depression marked by introversion, a perpetually gloomy outlook, and an apparent inability to experience much joy or pleasure from life. Dysthymics often are sluggish and have low self-esteem. The disorder is twice as likely to occur in women as in men. *Cyclothymia* is also a chronic mental condition that often becomes a way of life. A cyclothymic will never go for more than a few months without a phase of moderate manic or depressed behavior. Often they come to depend upon the manic periods, which are full of intense bursts of energy and heightened creative and mental acuity.

*Treatment.* Lithium is the drug of choice for those who suffer from bipolar disorder, although it doesn't work for everyone. Lithium is not used to correct an existing state of mania but rather to prevent future occurrences. Most physicians prescribe it in conjunction with another antipsychotic drug that is used to control the current manic attack. Lithium has common side effects, however, including weight gain, lethargy, twitches, nausea, hand tremor, and vertigo. It can also affect the thyroid and the kidneys, so the patient must be monitored regularly.

Two new medications are now being used to treat bipolar personalities: valproate (Depakote) and carbamazepine (Tegretol). Used for more than a decade for treating epilepsy, these medications do not cause cognitive impairment (one of the possible side effects of lithium), but they may have other serious side effects. Nevertheless, these two drugs are viable alternatives for people who cannot tolerate lithium's side effects.

## SUICIDAL THOUGHTS

Severely depressed people often have thoughts of committing suicide. Although these thoughts may not be necessarily connected to actual plans to end one's life, they are a common symptom of major depression and center around a person's feeling that life is not worth living and they see no future for themselves. Because thoughts of suicide are the most serious symptom—and sometimes outcome—of clinical depression, people expressing these wishes must be taken seriously. Physicians often will not raise the issue of suicide for fear of introducing the idea to the patient, so it is important to inform the physician if suicide has been mentioned by the patient. In fact, asking a patient if she has thought about suicide and if she has a plan can relieve this preoccupation and lessen the chances of suicide. Furthermore, asking the patient what would keep her from committing suicide can be lifesaving.

The elderly suffer most from depression-induced suicide. Often an older person's low spirits are confused with senile dementia and polypharmacy (the prescription and self-medication of too many medications) and the underlying depression goes untreated. Suicide is also more common among those suffering from alcoholism and those who live alone. Suicide is one of the nation's primary causes of adolescent death, and its incidence is on the rise. The rate of suicide among the elderly is three times that of adolescents. Women make far more attempts to kill themselves, but men are more likely to die from the act because they choose more lethal methods, such as a gun. Unfortunately in recent years women are also choosing more lethal methods. It is impossible to know for sure if a person who threatens suicide is actually serious about dying. If you know someone who has expressed a suicide wish, don't criticize or dismiss the behavior. Instead, make contact with a suicide hotline, a physician, or your local hospital. Wait until the depressed individual is under a physician's care before you leave her alone.

# DISSOCIATIVE DISORDERS

The dissociative disorders all involve disconnections of the personality, which means that at times memory for certain events, identity, and ability to handle situations are missing from the conscious mind. The person has usually suffered severe abuse in the past and learned to run away in her mind when she couldn't in actuality. The most common dissociative disorders are dissociative identity and dissociative amnesia.

## Dissociative Identity Disorder

Dissociative identity disorder, formerly called multiple personality disorder, is characterized by the existence of two or more personalities in the same individual, each with her own memories, experiences, behavioral patterns, and relationships. The number of different personalities existing in one body has been documented to range from two to one hundred, although more than half of these cases involve fewer than 10. Not as rare as once thought, dissociative identity disorder almost invariably develops in childhood. It is often the result of sexual abuse or severe trauma and is usually not diagnosed until years later. Women are more likely to have the disorder than men, and it is more common in those who are related to others with the disorder.

## Dissociative Amnesia

Not to be confused with the amnesia due to a general medical condition, dissociative amnesia is a loss of memory caused by a sudden shock or traumatic event. There are four forms of this type of amnesia.

- *Localized amnesia*—All of the events during a particular time frame are erased.

- *Selective amnesia*—Only certain experiences during a period of time are blocked out.

- *Generalized amnesia*—An entire life's past is forgotten.

- *Continuous amnesia*—All events following a certain period of time are blocked out, along with experiences that occur after the amnesia has begun.

Another form of amnesia is called *dissociative fugue.* This fairly rare condition occurs when a person assumes a completely new identity, forgetting the old one completely. While most with generalized amnesia may wander around confused, not knowing who they are, the person with dissociative fugue pursues her or his new existence with complete confidence and certainty.

*Treatment:* Generally, treatment for persons suffering from dissociative disorders involves support and psychotherapy with experienced therapists. Patients are encouraged to remember as much of their past as possible and to make the necessary adjustments to their present condition.

# PERSONALITY DISORDERS

Problems of the personality often are the result of unresolved emotional problems experienced during childhood. Many people exhibiting the symptoms of a personality disorder fail to seek treatment, preferring instead to blame others for their persistent difficulties in marriage, work, and relationships. Psychotherapy is the treatment of choice for these problems, although occasionally medications are also used. Generally, the following disorders reflect a person's inability to exist within the limitations and demands of the outside world.

## Avoidant Personality Disorder

Individuals with avoidant personality disorder withdraw socially. They may want to experience close relationships but fear rejection. People with avoidant personalities usually suffer from low self-esteem and tend to blame themselves for their social failures.

## Borderline Personality Disorder

People with borderline personality disorder have a poor self-image. They have unstable personal relationships, tending to focus on erratic or intense friendships. Extremely fearful of abandonment, these individuals suffer from frequent mood changes, a lack of inner control, anger, and an inclination to fight. Their self-damaging, impulsive behavior, sometimes accompanied by drug abuse, casual sex, and binge eating, usually estranges these people from peers and family. Recent research has shown that for many diagnosed with borderline personality disorder, their behavior is a consequence of underlying post-traumatic stress disorder consequent to abuse.

## Dependent Personality Disorder

As the name indicates, people with dependent personality disorder tend to depend on others to make the major decisions in their lives. Most common in domestically abused women, the disorder is closely linked with a fear of abandonment. A woman suffering from this syndrome can easily fall into a no-win cycle of asking her partner for advice on every aspect of her life, then finding she suffers from low self-esteem and depression because of her lack of independence.

## Histrionic Personality Disorder

More common in women than men, histrionic personality disorder is manifested by an exaggerated display of emotion. These people often display an overwrought and inappropriate demeanor in order to get the attention they crave. They may appear to be lively and warm at first meeting, but their relationships with others deteriorate swiftly as they become increasingly demanding and needy. Constantly seeking attention and praise, these individuals have a low frustration tolerance.

# Narcissistic Personality Disorder

The narcissist combines a sense of grandiose self-importance with bouts of inferiority. These people tend to brag about themselves while constantly checking what others think of them. People with this disorder demand full attention but are indifferent to the emotions and needs of others. If they are rejected, they tend to display excessive anger and envy.

# Obsessive-Compulsive Personality Disorder

People with obsessive-compulsive personality disorder spend most of their energy cultivating a sense of efficiency. They make lists and follow self-imposed rules, but they usually end up accomplishing very little. Preoccupied with the details of a trip, for example, an obsessive-compulsive will spend so much time worrying about the itinerary that she fails to enjoy the trip itself. Because of their excessive preoccupation with details, these people often spoil the experiences of people close to them.

# Paranoid Personality Disorder

People with paranoid personality disorder are overly suspicious and sensitive to perceived injuries and slights from others. They frequently blame others for their difficulties and have an exaggerated sense of their own importance. They appear cold and humorless, may show a limited range of emotional expression, and turn hostile if their defects are pointed out to them.

## Passive-Aggressive Personality Disorder

Passive-aggressive people tend to avoid doing whatever is expected of them, but without honestly refusing to do the particular task. Such a person will agree to take the responsibility for a job and then will proceed to fail. Tending to have difficulties at work and in intimate relationships, passive-aggressive individuals infuriate others with their lack of follow-through. They prefer to use procrastination and inefficiency to avoid their responsibilities, rather than openly expressing their frustrations or desires.

## Schizoid Personality Disorder

Individuals with schizoid personalities prefer social isolation. They have a difficult time experiencing or expressing warmth or intimate feelings. These people may be quite successful in their careers, but they tend to be solitary and completely involved in their own world.

## Schizotypal Personality Disorder

This group expresses schizophrenic symptoms in specific areas while appearing normal in other situations. For example, a person with a schizotypal personality might display strange mannerisms, speech patterns, or perceptions, but she will not be so out of touch with reality to be classified as a person who is schizophrenic.

*Treatment:* People suffering from personality disorders need the supportive counseling of experienced

## SOMATOFORM DISORDERS

The term *somatoform* refers to physical ailments that are either caused or strongly influenced by your emotions and current mental state. The label *psychosomatic* often has a negative connotation, implying that the illness is a product of your imagination rather than an actual ailment. To you, however, the pain and discomfort of a migraine, a skin rash, or an intestinal problem are real enough for you to seek relief and medical help.

Although the nature of somatoform illness is still not clearly understood, it is currently accepted in all of medicine that psychological factors can influence genetically predisposed people to succumb to a particular ailment or disease. For example, migraine attacks and eczema outbreaks—both diseases with genetic roots—are often triggered by fatigue and stress. If you have an illness that does not respond to standard medical therapy, your physician may ask you questions about your lifestyle and current frame of mind and life experiences. It is possible that counseling, relaxation techniques, and medications may help to lessen your symptoms and reduce the frequency of your attacks.

mental health professionals. The most common form of therapy is cognitive, but individual therapists may use a variety of methods. Many types of qualified therapists are available if you think you or someone you know needs counseling. Ask your physician for a referral, or call the local branch of the American Psychiatric Association for a list of professionals in your area. Help also may be obtained through community mental health clinics, family service centers, or from the referral services of a nearby hospital. Check your insurance coverage first, however; you may find that your policy has limitations on mental health coverage, and your insurance company may prefer that you use short-term therapy rather than traditional long-term psychotherapeutic treatment.

# SCHIZOPHRENIA

Schizophrenia—literally "split mind"—is a psychotic condition that severely impairs a person's social and psychological functioning. Difficult to treat and often chronic, schizophrenia is characterized by social withdrawal, unusual speech patterns, bizarre thoughts, and eccentric behavior. The schizophrenic is unable to differentiate between reality and delusion, and auditory hallucinations are common. Unable to respond rationally to a situation, the schizophrenic may laugh when the appropriate response is to cry. The schizophrenic is indifferent to her physical surroundings, may dress or groom eccentrically, and often has a bewildered, disheveled appearance.

Current research indicates that schizophrenia is caused by neurobiologic defects. The abnormal brain chemistry, and possibly, brain structure, that cause the disease can be inherited—but is not always. Equally common in both sexes, schizophrenia usually appears during adolescence and early adulthood and at times of great stress or loss. Onset is later in women, who also experience fewer hospitalizations, respond better to hospitalizations, and have better relationships with their families. Schizophrenia has some variations:

- People with *paranoid* schizophrenia have delusions of persecution, believing that they will be poisoned, attacked, or destroyed by others, or that people are stealing their ideas and using them for their own ends. They may hear voices and talk to voices in their minds which may tell them to commit certain actions.

- *Catatonic* schizophrenics usually alternate between bouts of extreme excitability and stupor. Often they remain mute and apparently unseeing for long periods of time, although they may be aware of what is going on around them.

- *Disorganized* schizophrenics are usually incoherent, displaying inappropriate and bizarre emotions and actions. At other times, they are expressionless and non-reactive.

People who suffer acute or severe episodes of schizophrenia must be treated in the hospital. Electroconvulsive therapy is used in some cases, but antipsychotic drugs are usually prescribed to reduce the person's agitation and lessen the psychotic symptoms. These drugs, called major tranquilizers, are used to treat patients suffering from a variety of psychoses, including schizophrenia, mania, medically caused disorders, and thought disorders caused by drug and alcohol abuse.

The antipsychotic drugs work by blocking the receptors in the brain that are linked by the nerve chemical dopamine. Chlorpromazine (Thorazine) and haloperidol (Haldol) are especially effective in treating people suffering from a psychotic episode. Side effects are numerous, however, including dry mouth, constipation, loss of bladder control, sexual difficulties, blurred vision, tremors, and an involuntary facial movement called tardive dyskinesia. These side effects are usually directly related to the dosage and the length of time the patient is on the drug. Altering the dosage frequently alleviates most of these problems. There are medications like benztropine mesylate (Cogentin) that can lessen some of these extrapyramidal symptoms. However, for tardive dyskinesia, you must discontinue the drug and wait— sometimes for several months—for the symptoms possibly to subside.

Some people will experience an episode of schizophrenia and later return to normal with the knowledge that they will relapse again with the same symptoms. In those instances, the most effective treatment is the administration of drugs to change the brain chemistry; this type of therapy usually lasts up to six months. Others, however, may suffer from severe chronic episodes of schizophrenia and require continued medication to maintain even a semblance of a normal life. In both cases, supportive psychotherapy can be used to help the patient and family and significant others understand and control the life stresses that may trigger an attack.

# MENTAL DISORDERS DUE TO A GENERAL MEDICAL CONDITION

Mental confusion and disorientation can also be caused by a physical illness or infection that in turn influences brain function. Organic mental disorders are best treated by dealing with the physical problem first, which can include cerebral infection, brain trauma, vascular accidents (stroke), brain tumors, degenerative disorders, nutritional deficiencies, endocrine disorders, and epilepsy. Although the cause of these mental disturbances tends to be an illness, the condition can also be the result of toxic chemicals and withdrawal from drugs and alcohol.

## Symptoms and Diagnosis

The symptoms of these disorders are strikingly similar to those of psychogenic disorders, involving:

- impaired intellectual comprehension
- impaired speech patterns
- inability to calculate simple numbers
- faulty memory
- inappropriate decisions or judgment
- rapid mood swings
- general disorientation.

Endocrine disorders are a good example of how an organic disturbance in the brain can result in a loss of normal intellectual functioning and behavior. The endocrine glands—especially the thyroid and adrenal glands—are responsible for producing hormones in the body that affect energy level, growth and development, and sexual functioning. A hyperactive thyroid or hyperthyroidism (called Graves' disease) is characterized by agitation, hallucinations, sweating, and other symptoms of acute anxiety. An underactive thyroid, on the other hand, may lead to myxedema, which in turn can lead to episodes of severe depression. Hyperactivity of the adrenal glands (Cushing's syndrome), is characterized by severe mood swings, general weakness, and obesity. Underactivity of the adrenal glands may cause Addison's disease, which can cause acute depression and/or anxiety. People with diabetes often experience depression.

# SLEEP DISORDERS

Getting a good night's sleep is extremely important to our daily functioning and to our general mental and physical health. But a good night's sleep varies for different people—some require up to nine hours while others can do quite nicely with six. A middle-aged adult, however, usually needs at least $7^1/2$ hours of sleep a night to feel good the next day. If you don't get your required amount of sleep, you'll feel tired, less alert, and less efficient. A chronic lack of sleep—whether because of shift work, jet lag, or just watching too much television—can severely impair your judgment and lead to accidents at home, on the job, and on the road.

# Insomnia

Occasionally you may experience difficulties falling asleep. Your wakefulness may be the result of a stressful day, sleeping in a strange bed, or apprehension before an exam or starting a new job. Short-term insomnia that lasts for a number of days may be caused by a death in the family, difficulties in a relationship, or worry over financial matters. Chronic or persistent insomnia may last for many weeks or months. It may stem from depression, overuse of alcohol and caffeine, or a reliance on sleep medications.

*Treatment:* If you have chronic difficulty falling asleep at night, the first step is to make certain changes in your bedtime routine that may help you fall asleep.

- Avoid strenuous exercise before bedtime. Regular exercise during the day is beneficial for sleep, but exercise right before going to bed has the opposite effect of too much stimulation instead of relaxation.

- Don't drink tea, coffee, or soft drinks containing caffeine for at least four to six hours before bedtime. Also avoid alcoholic drinks. The alcohol may make you fall asleep faster, but it can also disrupt normal sleeping patterns and result in awakening during the night.

- Refrain from napping during the day, if possible. Habitual napping can disrupt your need for sleep at night.

- Be cautious about your use of over-the-counter and prescription sleeping medications. It's all too easy to develop a dependence on these drugs, with a corresponding disruption in your normal sleeping patterns. And most of these medications lose their effectiveness after 4 to 6 weeks.

- Relax in the evening before you go to bed. Restrict your reading and TV watching to lighter fare, and avoid emotionally upsetting topics right before bedtime. Try not to worry about what you have to do the next day.

- Make sure your physical surroundings are con-

## CHANGING SLEEP PATTERNS

Sleep patterns vary considerably according to your age. Newborns sleep five or six times during the day, while the older child takes one or two daily naps in addition to sleeping through the night. Young adults, on the average, need at least seven to eight hours of sleep a night. Pregnancy can temporarily impair sleep because of hormonal changes. However, no medications must be used.

In later years—sometime after age 60—you may notice a tendency to return to frequent daytime naps and to less sleep at night. Instead of the continuous period of sleep you had been accustomed to, you may experience less deep sleep and more frequent awakenings. Your "insomnia," in that case, may simply be a normal adaptation to changing sleep patterns that occur with advancing years.

ducive to sleep. The room should be sufficiently darkened, and the temperature should be comfortable. People who work at home should avoid using their bedroom as an office; it may help if you can screen off that part of the room from the area around your bed.

■ Don't try to force sleep. If you find yourself tossing and turning, get up and read or watch television until you feel sleepy. Try a glass of skim milk.

If all else fails, you may need the advice of a professional sleep expert to solve your chronic sleep problems. First, though, have a careful medical evaluation to determine if there is a physical component to your sleeplessness.

## Sleep Apnea

A potentially serious disorder, apnea is characterized by recurrent halts in breathing, loud snoring, and deep gasps for breath. People suffering from this disorder often wake with a headache and feel tired and irritable during the day. More men than women suffer from sleep apnea, especially if they are overweight. At its worst, the lack of oxygen during the cessation of breathing could cause a heart arrhythmia or even a heart attack. Treatment may call for weight reduction, medication, or the use of a machine that delivers continuous air flow through a mask. Surgery to open the air passages is a last resort; this procedure has not been particularly successful in eliminating the apnea.

## Restless Leg Syndrome

Sometimes, lying in bed at night, you may experience unpleasant creeping sensations deep inside your leg. This feeling forces you to move your legs in a jerking or kicking motion. You may have to get out of bed and

---

## DUAL DIAGNOSES

Especially in the last two decades, the incidence of dual diagnosis has gained in importance as a result of research. Dual diagnosis means that a woman is suffering from a substance abuse disorder and another major mental illness such as major depressive disorder, bipolar disorder, or schizophrenia. Treating one illness alone when two exist understandably leads to treatment failure. Therefore it is extremely important that, without shame or guilt, women patients tell their physicians, and other health professionals treating them, that they have an addiction problem as well as an emotional, psychological, or psychiatric illness. Although the exact etiology is unknown, lesbians suffer from alcoholism to a greater extent than heterosexual women. Clearly societal pressures and discrimination can be involved. There are increasing numbers of treatment centers for people, and many specifically for women, with dual diagnoses. When properly recognized, treatment success rates are high and women recover to go on with better lives.

walk around to relieve the symptoms. Sometimes your feet, thighs, and arms may also be affected. The causes of restless leg syndrome are not clear, although the syndrome often appears during times of stress. The disorder can stem from a neuropathy associated with diabetes, or from some mineral deficiency. Restless leg syndrome is not dangerous, but the sensations involved are uncomfortable and annoying, and can disrupt sleep. If your physician can't give you relief, you may want to consult a sleep specialist or a sleep clinic for diagnosis and treatment.

# EATING DISORDERS

The act of eating has long been thought of as a crucial part of the psychological development of the human being. Many mental health professionals believe that a healthy attitude toward food symbolizes the security of feeling loved, while an abnormal anxiety about eating may reflect inner conflicts, a basic insecurity, and low self-esteem. There also may be physiological problems involved that are as yet poorly understood.

## Obesity

Obesity is a controversial topic today because severely overweight people are often made to feel responsible for their condition and suffer social stigma as a result. Recent research has shown that obesity—the state of exceeding ideal weight by more than 20 percent—is not always caused by excessive eating. Activity levels and the metabolic rate at which calories are burned are two factors affecting the creation of excessive fat in the body. Some people are more prone to gain weight than others because of their genetically determined metabolic rate.

Obesity is a health risk, however. Excess fat can affect the liver and increase the risk of diabetes. Extra fat may also be associated with higher triglyceride blood fat levels and increased risk of heart disease and heart attacks. Hypertension, too, occurs three times more frequently in overweight people, and can lead to stroke. Cancers of the colon, rectum, gallbladder, ovary, cervix, and breast also tend to occur more frequently in women who are obese.

Many obese individuals could lose weight by implementing a more careful diet and by exercising

## SLEEP CLINICS

Many large medical centers and hospitals have sleep clinics for the diagnosis of sleep disorders. You enter the clinic during the day and spend a few nights there for a complete sleep diagnosis and evaluation. A variety of tests are performed to measure your body movement during sleep, your brain waves, the level of oxygen in your blood, and your heart and breathing rates. The results of the tests will allow a specialist in sleep disorders to pinpoint the cause of your insomnia and to offer an appropriate treatment.

more. However, dieting is not the final answer. Chronic dieting can cause repeated weight loss and gain—a phenomenon known as the yo-yo syndrome. This syndrome slows down metabolism and makes it harder to lose weight the next time around. The best solution is behavior modification. This means gradually changing your eating habits and increasing your physical activity.

## Anorexia Nervosa and Bulimia

Two common eating disorders—anorexia nervosa and bulimia—can be especially dangerous. Anorectics begin by showing an exaggerated interest in food—counting calories, baking for the family—but gradually eat less and less themselves. They diet excessively and often exercise to the point of near-exhaustion before someone else notices their emaciated physical condition and their abnormal fear of gaining weight. Bulimics, on the other hand, consume large amounts of food periodically—so-called binge eating—and then force themselves to vomit the food. Bulimics also have a great fear of getting fat, although most are in the normal weight range for their height.

In 85 to 95 percent of cases, anorexia and bulimia affect young women, often beginning in the teenage years. The specific causes of anorexia and bulimia are not known, although it is thought that several factors play a role in their development, including a biologic predisposition to the disease, social pressures to be slim, family disturbances and conflicts, and a fear of sexuality. Both anorexia and bulimia are serious diseases and call for immediate treatment. Severe and long-term anorexia can lead to extreme emaciation and even death. Bulimia can have serious health consequences by depleting the body of water and potassium and can also result in death from cardiac arrhythmia.

*Treatment:* Both disorders are difficult to treat, and relapses are common. In severe cases, hospitalization is necessary to control weight and to eliminate dangerous practices, such as vomiting and the abuse of laxatives and diuretics. In many cases, psychological counseling and diet counseling can help control the anorectic's abnormal eating habits. Bulimics usually respond to psychotherapy and behavioral therapy. Women suffering from eating disorders can also find sympathy and support in self-help groups and from group therapy.

# PART II
# Staying Healthy in Spite of Stress

Jeanne Spurlock, M.D., F.A.P.A.

**P**erhaps you already understand the familiar price that stress can exact: those butterflies in your stomach, the trouble concentrating, a feeling of being overwhelmed, pressured, or tense. It may start as something minor: You've worked all day in an office, behind a counter, or in a factory trying to please supervisors who don't understand the limitations of time. Finally, you are at home. The phone rings. You are trying to unpack eight bags of groceries. The children are hungry. Laundry baskets of unwashed clothes catch your eye. Your husband is calling to tell you that he will be late. At 6:00 P.M. in a messy kitchen, you feel your life is horribly disorganized and out of your control. You notice that you are breathing in short, uneven gasps. Your head starts throbbing. Your hands get cold. An imaginary band running across your shoulders tightens its grip on your muscles. Your tension is creating more tension. As a woman living in the 1990s, you may know these feelings only too well. This is clearly demonstrated in the following vignettes.

Eileen is a 38-year-old graphics designer for a major catalog company in New York City. Recently, at the end of a long, pressure-filled day, she excused herself from a meeting, walked to the ladies' room down the hall, and threw up. It wasn't the flu that had upset her stomach.

At age 22, with no previous cardiac symptoms, Karen thought she was having a heart attack. As a college senior carrying 22 credits, Karen was also playing in a concert band, working for the school newspaper, helping her sorority, and serving on the board of several honor societies. It was too much to do. "My chest got very heavy. I couldn't breathe," she recalls. "It was so painful. I got myself to the infirmary and the doctor there said, 'You are having a panic attack.'"

Dorothy, 44, feels as if she is in a pressure cooker with a busy ophthalmologic practice, six children, and a husband. She races from office visits with patients to the supermarket for groceries and barely suppresses the daily rise of panic about carrying out her carpool assignments and meeting professional deadlines. Feeling guilty, exhausted, and continuously hassled, Dorothy wouldn't dare put herself first "no matter how pressed I am for time to unwind."

When she was 57, Josephine found herself sitting in her surgeon's office listening to her plans to operate on Josephine's wrists in order to relieve the pain of an arthritic condition. She had been working as a nurse in her state's sexually transmitted disease unit, and each day on the job brought more stress and less movement in her hands. "I couldn't even comb my hair without propping my elbows on a bureau," she recalls. Instead of surgery, however, Jo accepted early retirement. Within three months, her disabling symptoms disappeared.

Mary, a 55-year-old widow, has assumed the responsibility of caring for three grandchildren, ages 6, 4, and 14 months, in order to prevent their placement in foster care. Mary's daughter, a known substance abuser for nearly a year, was charged with neglect and abuse. Mary's anger about the situation was quickly replaced with guilt, and then the somatic symptoms surfaced.

Stress can make you sick. Doctors know this to be true, although patients don't always want to make such a mind-body connection. In study after study, the medical research in the last forty years has proven just how physically demanding and potentially life-threatening chronic stress really is, especially for women.

Stress is simply part of the human condition. In fact, a certain amount of daily pressure is absolutely normal and can make you more alert, more vibrant, and more motivated to reach your goals. Women often thrive in busy environments. For too many women today, however, this ordinary level of stress is exceeded every day. As emotional and physical caretakers for many people in their lives, some women insist on pushing themselves from morning until night assuming a multitude of traditional roles while coping with a job and financial responsibilities that often conflict with parenting and home.

The link between your brain and body is very direct, and neither you nor your physician can afford to separate your physical complaints from your emotional equilibrium. Medicine has made dramatic advances in caring for and curing some of the problems of acute infectious diseases, but now we need to turn our attention to what appears to have become an epidemic of female stress-induced illness.

# HOW STRESS AFFECTS THE BODY

Although individual physical and emotional reactions to stress vary, the results are similar. A stress overload activates areas of your brain that then send involuntary impulses to organs elsewhere in your body. You can blame your general adaptation reflex—an involuntary series of physical reactions—as well as your ancestors for your biological inability to handle excess stress without getting sick. When you become frightened, your body switches into its emergency "fight or flight" mode. This is a completely natural, normal response involving your endocrine system, your autonomic nervous system, the hypothalamus in your brain, and your limbic system.

## What the Hypothalamus Does

The size of a grape, your hypothalamus takes care of a multitude of responsibilities. (See Fig. 2.1) Located in the center of your brain and linked to your pituitary gland, it stores hormones and reigns over your endocrine system, the network of glands all over your body. The hypothalamus sends messages to your nervous system and communicates directly with its neighbors in the brain. You can envision this structure as the ultimate link between your mind and body. The hypothalamus turns on the tap of your physical sensations when you respond to something emotional, whether in fear, love, anger, frustration, or anxiety. These intangible sensations soon become quite tangible as your body reacts.

**Figure 2.1.** Functions of the Hypothalamus

The hypothalamus is the part of the brain linked to the pituitary or "master" gland. The hypothalamus causes the release of hormones to the pituitary, which in turn triggers the release of other hormones into the bloodstream. These hormones, produced by glands throughout the body, affect growth, metabolism, and all aspects of reproduction. The ovary, thyroid gland, and adrenal cortex are under the control of the pituitary gland. The hypothalamus and pituitary cause the mammary glands to begin producing milk after birth. Hormones also affect bone strength and can cause muscles to become tense during stressful situations.

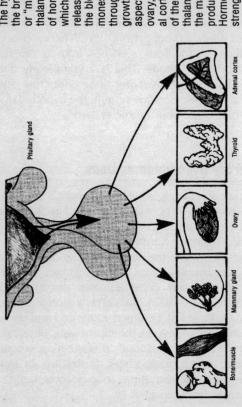

Pituitary gland

Bone/muscle    Mammary gland    Ovary    Thyroid    Adrenal cortex

Some researchers have called the hypothalamus "the master gland" because it produces at least nine different hormones triggering almost all of the other glands in your body to swing into action or quiet down. Extreme fear, for example, affects the body in many different ways. Your pupils will widen to let in more light. You will experience an increase in alertness. Your adrenal glands will begin to pump more adrenaline and other hormones into your bloodstream. Your heart races, your blood pressure rises, your muscles tense. Your liver starts converting starches to sugars for energy. Digestion slows. Experts have even determined that your blood's clotting powers will be enhanced during stressful situations. Sweat production increases and the hair on your body may feel prickly and actually stand on end. All these physical reactions were designed to save your life. Your body is getting ready to defend itself. But these reactions are no longer physiologically useful in modern life and can actually be harmful if you keep yourself in such an alert state for too many hours each day.

Not surprisingly, a daily regimen of racing heartbeat, pulsing blood, tensed muscles, undigested food stuck in your stomach, and elevated levels of hormones coursing through your circulatory system poses all kinds of potential health problems. Take the hormone cortisol, for instance. It is released under stress to inhibit inflammation at the site of any potential wounds, yet it is unlikely that you will need the assistance of cortisol. Your boss isn't really going to inflict bodily harm on you if you can't finish the paperwork on your desk. He or she may scream or fume or threaten disciplinary action, of course, but that cortisol coursing through your veins, getting ready to heal cuts, abrasions, or bruises from a real fight, isn't helping you at all. In fact, it's hurting you, because cortisol can boost your blood pressure and lead to hypertension.

Too much stress also affects your immune system, weakening it and making you more susceptible to colds, coughs, and infections. It has been traced as the culprit in flareups of arthritis and asthma. Your urinary tract can also be affected. There is a natural balance of friendly and unfriendly organisms that normally co-exist in our digestive and urinary systems. Constant anxiety can destroy this immunological balance, however, leading to an overgrowth of the harmful bacteria and an infection.

## Why Women Are So Vulnerable

While it is true that men may face more immediate life-threatening occupational hazards, women appear to be more vulnerable to stress-induced illnesses, for a variety of reasons. First, they are socialized to be caretakers, and as such they almost automatically take on responsibilities that men might not even consider. This alone adds to the stress loads they carry. Second, women as a whole are less likely to be in positions of power and are not as able to control what's going on in their environment as most men. If you can't say no, the stress you feel can be doubly disastrous because you don't see any escape. The less power you have over the circumstances of your everyday existence, the heavier the stress load.

It may be obvious that what complicates a woman's stress is work. Men who are stretched thin at their work places often go home to relax. Women, on the other hand, go home and keep on working. In spite of the increasing number of women with careers and jobs, traditional roles in their homes still take precedence for many women. They can expect to be in charge of everything from child care to laundry, food preparation, social calendars, and runny noses. Delegating these duties to others in their households helps, but in the long run most women are still in charge. Given this situation, their minds as well as their bodies work overtime. When they become

## THE PSYCHOLOGICAL SIGNS OF STRESS

Ask yourself the following questions:

- Are you nervous, anxious?
- Do you feel depressed or sad?
- Are you irritable or moody?
- Do you often become frustrated?
- Are you forgetful?
- Do you have trouble thinking clearly?
- Can you make decisions without agonizing?
- Is it difficult to learn new information?
- Do you have insomnia?
- Are you plagued by negative thoughts?
- Are you fidgety?
- Are you accident-prone?
- Do you bite your fingernails or cuticles?

angry about too much to do in too little time with too little help, the anger only adds to their overstressed physical condition. Even women who sense their own need to slow down are programmed toward overcommitment because they feel guilty about not being able to be everything to everyone in their lives.

## THE PHYSICAL SYMPTOMS OF STRESS

These symptoms, if chronic, may be signs of extreme anxiety and stress. They may also relate to a physical disorder. If they are sudden, severe, or persist, see your doctor.

- Back pain
- Muscle tension
- Headaches
- Trembling hands
- Diarrhea
- Constipation
- Pounding heart
- Chest pain
- Sweaty, cold hands
- Shortness of breath
- Indigestion or gas pains
- Burping
- A burning sensation in your chest
- Feeling faint or dizzy
- A lingering head cold
- Ringing in the ears
- Grinding your teeth
- Hives or skin rashes
- Loss of appetite
- Feeling nauseated, vomiting
- Pain in your stomach

Time spent alone or nurturing their own mental and physical well-being might be construed as selfish, so they push even harder on all fronts—home, work, and social. Sociologists speculate that many women today may be disadvantaged because they have incorporated a male standard for achievement in the work world with an old-fashioned female standard for perfection at home.

# HOW TO COPE WITH STRESS

To get some control into your life and tame the stress that could be making you sick, a two-way approach is recommended. First, it is necessary to change your behavior so you can slow the emotional pace of your life. Second, learn how to turn off your general adaptation reflex. You can do this by using exercise and relaxation techniques.

## How to Change Your Behavior

*Allow yourself regular leisure time.* Leisure time is a necessity, not a reward for having completed all your tasks. Deep psychic benefits come from forgetting your chores and what time it is. For example, take a magazine into the bathroom, fill the tub, climb in, and relax. The leisurely soak will give you the strength to do more later. Take an hour or half hour to be by yourself each day. Many highly successful people have discovered that a key to keeping their minds sharp and their bodies healthy is to sit quietly and daydream a little each day. If sitting still makes you feel anxious or guilty, browse in a bookstore, walk around the block, or find some other undemanding yet pleasurable activity. A caution, however: Even leisure activities offer little refreshment if you run through them, squeezing in a quick bath, a little tennis, racing to the fast-food restaurant with kids, or are always considering what must be done next. The key is to plan—don't wait for free time to suddenly appear. The only way to create time for yourself is to take it away from some other activity. Personal time for refueling and staying healthy will never be available unless you plan for it purposefully.

*Set goals for yourself.* This may mean reordering your daily priorities. When you give a little of yourself to everything, you commit a great deal of yourself to nothing. Think back to the days when you have been most fragmented. Were you trying to complete an impossibly long list of things to do? If you work, try to take work breaks that remove you physically or mentally from the office. If possible, don't take office work home with you.

*Insist on help with regular chores.* Learn how to delegate without guilt. Basic changes aimed at lightening your load can ease your stress considerably. Pick something in your life that you find hard to ignore—unmade beds, dirty dishes—and ask for help. If something can be ignored, however, let it be until you have more leisure time to tackle that particular chore. Don't be a perfectionist.

When you start to delegate items on your "to do" list, decide on tasks (1) that you can give to someone else, (2) that others (especially kids) can do for themselves, (3) that you're doing out of habit, (4) that are low priority and a waste of your energy, and (5) that you are only doing to please others or to make them feel guilty. In the meantime, when you feel pressed for time, ask yourself, What will happen if I don't do this project? You may be surprised to find out how many chores can easily be dropped without any repercussions or anyone even noticing.

*Don't combine too many activities.* Some women can't resist the urge to talk on the telephone, reshuffle the daily demands clipped to their desk or kitchen counters, and cook a meal all at the same time. They may be experts at combining activities, and most of the time this ability gives them a great sense of satisfaction. However, one of the reasons many women end up feeling stressed is that they feel fragmented, worn down, and weary from having to respond to too many people and situations. Occasionally slowing down to focus on one thing is essential to keeping your emotions and those of the people around you balanced. If you really want to enjoy a meal or a conversation with someone, it is important to concentrate on that activity to the exclusion of everything else.

*Take advantage of your natural body rhythms.* There may be 24 hours in a day, but your mood and energy level can't keep up with the clock all day. The sooner you figure out when your prime time is, the less overwhelmed you will feel. Most people are at their peak between 10:00 A.M. and 2:00 P.M., but you know your own body best. By adjusting your routine slightly you may be able to eliminate some of the stress from your life. For example, save routine tasks for periods when your energy is at its lowest point. Devote your peak hours to more demanding or enjoyable projects.

*Stop running to answer every request.* A ringing telephone, a doorbell, or the sudden demand of an impatient co-worker makes some women jump, no matter what else they have been doing. Even in midbite, midsentence, or midnap, you may feel obliged to answer all such calls for your immediate presence. Some experts believe that women who have trouble managing stress operate under the tyranny of believing that these demands on their life are always important. Often they are not. In fact, the really important matters in life don't always appear to be urgent. Prioritizing doesn't mean shirking your responsibilities. It does mean making a conscious effort to separate what's important from what's merely "urgent" at the time. Think first: Is this *really* important, or could it be done later? Then give your attention to the things that really count.

*Learn how to say no.* For many women, turning down someone who asks for a chunk of your time is never easy. It is nice to be needed, but adding extra burdens can wreak havoc on your day. These suggestions may help. (1) Say no fast, before they can anticipate a yes. Hedging with "I don't know" or "Let me think about it" only complicates your life, adding stress because you'll have to call back and beg off later. (2) Be as polite and pleasant as possible. (3) Offer a counterproposal. If you can't take on a complete responsibility for a new project, consider sharing with someone else or suggesting another person for the assignment.

*Look at time as your life.* When you stop trying to

spend, save, and invest time, you'll feel less stressed out. Of course, your time is important. It's your life, after all. By looking at it from such a mercenary, rushed, overstressed viewpoint, you may be missing out on much that is truly enjoyable as well as the activities and people that make life worth living.

*Locate the source of your stress.* Sometimes women don't stop to focus on exactly why they feel overwhelmed. If you can analyze your day's load of stress, you may be able to pinpoint a particular problem and be able to deal with the stress more effectively. For instance, the next time someone in your office hands you several projects simultaneously and each one is dubbed an emergency, think before you panic. Instead of agonizing alone, go back to your boss and ask which one should be done first, second, and third. The more information you can gather and the more support you can pull together, the easier it will be to cope with the stress.

## How to Turn Off the Physical Symptoms of Stress

You probably don't need medication or therapy to relieve the physical symptoms of stress. The first important step is simply to recognize the particular way you experience stress. The second step is to take any unwanted side effects seriously. Third, you need to learn how to turn off your body's "fight or flight" reflex by using breathing, exercise, or relaxation techniques. Use the following methods the next time you feel yourself being physically engulfed by stress.

*Breathe deeply.* Breathing is critical to dealing

with stress effectively. A lack of oxygen restricts blood flow and causes muscles to tense. When you are panicked, you tend to take short, shallow gasps of air, hardly using your diaphragm at all. Your chest muscles and the accessory breathing muscles in your shoulders are overloaded and do all the work of respiration. The next time you are in a stressful situation, (1) sit up straight, (2) inhale through your nose with your mouth closed, (3) exhale through your mouth with your lips pursed (as if you were whistling or kissing), (4) make your exhalation twice as long as your inhalation (inhale for two seconds, exhale for four, for instance). Use your abdomen when you breathe, consciously pushing your belly out. Try putting one hand over your stomach, in fact, to see how it rises and falls. You are allowing more air to enter your body, and in the process you will slow down your heart rate, lower your blood pressure, and eventually break the stress cycle.

*Practice progressive relaxation techniques.* Sit in a quiet spot and take off your shoes or any uncomfortable clothing, including eyeglasses. Close your eyes, uncross your legs, place your hands in your lap palms up, and let your head rest easily. (Lie down if you prefer.) Start by tightening the muscles in your feet and toes and then relaxing them. Gradually work this tightening and relaxing pattern up through your legs, back, chest, and head, including your face. Clench your jaws. Hold that tension. Then relax.

Another relaxation exercise is to picture yourself in a pleasant place. Perhaps it's a calm lake or a mountain view that puts your mind at rest. Visualize this scene in your mind as you slowly let each part of your body go limp. Breathe deeply. Aim for at least

10 minutes or more of progressive relaxation, if possible. To know if you are truly relaxed, feel the temperature of your hands. Warm hands mean a relaxed body. If your hands are still cool, you know you are still tense. (Put them on your neck to test the temperature.) Continue your relaxation until they warm up.

To get the most benefit from any relaxation technique, you'll have to practice it often. Choose a time of day when you won't be interrupted. Turn off the radio, TV, and stereo. If you learn how to switch into this relaxation mode in private, you'll be better able to do it under stress.

*Exercise your shoulders and neck muscles.* We store stress in the muscles of the upper back, shoulders, and neck. Learn how to release this tension by gently moving that area of the body. The movements don't have to be complicated. To loosen up the tightness:

- *Shrug your shoulders.* Stand up or sit. Hunch your shoulders up around your ears and tighten the muscles as much as possible. Let them drop and relax. Repeat.

- *Stretch up and overhead.* While sitting in a chair, bring your arms overhead, holding them straight with fingertips pointing toward the ceiling. Elbows shouldn't be locked. Reach skyward with your right hand and then with your left hand. You should feel the stretch, but nothing should hurt. Breathe comfortably throughout.

- *Swing your arms.* Stand up. Let your arms hang loose at your sides. Lean forward slightly and swing your arms back and forth and from side to side across your chest. Stop swinging. Relax and breathe deeply.

- *Walk.* Go out for a walk, but leave your purse behind; if you carry a bag, you might throw your body off balance. Walk briskly but don't race. Hurrying may make you lean forward unconsciously, creating tension in the curve of your shoulders. Throw your shoulders back, expand your chest area, and breathe deeply.

## LISTEN TO YOUR BODY

As our critical knowledge of the mind-body connection grows, it becomes even more apparent that you are your own best weapon in defending yourself against stress-related illness. Become a more active listener to the signals your own body may be sending. Don't deny or ignore symptoms of stress. A consultation with your doctor may be advisable. It may be that she will determine that the symptoms are indeed related to stress and reaffirm the importance of taking your leisure time seriously. If you aren't enjoying the responsibilities of your life, then you are probably overestimating your capacity to handle stress. It might be that the stress you experience at a particular time in your life is overwhelming. Don't be reticent about seeking professional help at those times. Such a move can be life-saving. So it was for Mary, the 55-year-old grandmother who was previously described. She arranged to see her doctor before her scheduled appointment. The doctor found Mary's blood pressure, previously controlled by medication, to be elevated to an alarming degree. The medication was changed, and a referral was made to a mental health facility for an evaluation. This referral led to a therapeutic encounter that enabled Mary to resolve her anger and guilt about her daughter and to explore the possibility for assistance from social agencies. Mary accepted the therapist's admonition that she couldn't be all things to all people.

# PART III
# Violence and Women

Marjorie Braude, M.D.

Stalking. Date rape. These are frightening new words that have been coined to describe violent offenses against women. Violence in all of its forms has become woven into the everyday fabric of our lives.

- Every 6 minutes a woman is raped.
- Every l5 seconds a woman is punched, slapped, kicked, or otherwise physically abused by a man she knows.
- Every day, approximately four women are murdered by their husbands or boyfriends.

These horrifying statistics point out that half of all American women experience violence from men at some point in their lives—often at the hands of husbands and lovers. Even if you have managed to escape violence yourself, you more than likely know someone who is a survivor of rape, sexual abuse, or battery. Violence can strike anywhere: it affects women of every class, ethnicity, and level of education, in rural villages, the suburbs, and in urban settings.

As if real life isn't threatening enough, much of our popular culture seems to encourage this pervasive climate of violence. From the pages of pornographic magazines with their scenes of brutal bondage to films and television programs depicting women who are stalked, terrorized, and tortured, women are viewed more often than not as helpless victims and men as ruthless aggressors. Even today's popular music—particularly rap—continues to assault our ears with denigrating lyrics about women who need to be taught to stay in their place.

Whether we are aware of it or not, the fear engendered in us by both the real and fictionalized images of violence affects our daily lives. Consider how it has affected and limited your own life. Are you afraid to go out alone at night? Are you cautious to the point of isolation? Have you joined the growing ranks of women who own and carry a weapon?

Unfortunately, as careful as we may be outside our homes, often it is from those within our closest circle that we have the most to fear. According to a 1992 report by the National Crime Victim Center, nearly eight out of ten rape survivors knew their attacker. Childhood sexual abuse occurs most often between a father or stepfather and a daughter, not with some evil lurking stranger. Domestic battery—injury of a women at the hands of her husband or lover—is responsible for more injuries to adult women than from any other cause, including car accidents and muggings combined.

## A GROWING CALL FOR ACTION

Despite the alarming statistics, there is some encouraging news. Clearly, no one simple antidote to violence against women exists, but people are working on all fronts to develop cures. Today more and more women are taking control of their own lives, as well as helping to work with others to stop the cycle of violence in their homes and on their streets. Crisis centers, shelters, and hotlines for rape and domestic abuse now exist all over the country. Classes in self-defense are increasingly being filled by women. Paradoxically, the media, besides being contributors to glorifying violence, are also its "unmaskers": By documenting the violence, the veil of secrecy and shame has been lifted from the faces of women who want to share their stories of surviving rape, childhood sexual abuse, and battery. Magazine articles, television shows, and documentaries are now covering gender-based violence, including how to recognize and protect against it and how to recover from it.

To some degree, the legal, political, and medical establishments have joined the media. Crimes against women are being taken more seriously than ever before. For example, restraining orders designed to protect battery victims from their abusers have recently been issued more often and more strictly enforced. New laws have been passed to cover crimes against women. For example, a 1993 study conducted by the Centers for Disease Control and Prevention showed that the incidence of stalking—that is, repeated harassment and surveillance with threats of violence—has rapidly increased; 48 states now have some form of anti-stalking laws that call for prison terms and fines. These laws have given the police more authority in an area where they previously had none.

On still another front, those in mainstream medicine, specialty societies, nursing, and other health professions have been urged to increase their responsibilities to those patients who are the survivors of abuse. Until recently, too often physicians never saw past the broken ribs or lacerated eyes to the underlying problem of domestic abuse. They put a Band-Aid on the problem by focusing only on treating the injuries and sending the abused woman back to her abuser. Today that picture is changing as more and more medical schools, residencies, and ongoing medical education forums are training physicians to recognize and treat survivors of gender-based violence.

# THE EFFECTS OF VIOLENCE ON WOMEN

All gender-based crime results in a special set of circumstances for its survivors. A common outcome is post-traumatic stress disorder (PTSD). Short-term or one-time assault can result in PTSD, as well as long-term effects of victimization.

Some women react to the stress of violence by experiencing repeated mental flashbacks. They are hypersensitive to their surroundings and react strongly to any event or location that reminds them of the trauma. Other women, rather than recalling the event, try to deny the incidents ever happened. Associated memories may begin to trickle in after some coincidental event; however, many women so successfully block the crime (particularly if they were victims of childhood sexual abuse) that it is only through long-term psychotherapy and/or judicious hypnosis that the event can be remembered at all. Perhaps worst of all, gender-based violence often results in the stripping of self-esteem and self-confidence. In fact, the survivor is often left blaming herself and not the perpetrator of the crime.

A woman who has experienced violence needs both immediate crisis support and intervention as well as long-term physical, psychological, legal, and social help. The particular challenges a woman faces depend to a large degree on the type of gender-based crime to which she is subjected.

# RAPE

According to statistics collected by the National Victim Center, about 683,000 women were raped—forced against their will into sexual acts—in the United States in 1990. Altogether, more than 12 million American women, or one in every eight, have been raped at some time in their lives.

The word *rape* comes from the Latin *rapere,* "to take by force." The traditional legal definition of rape in the United States is carnal knowledge (vaginal penetration) of a female through the use of force or the threat of force and without her consent. Most states have revised, or are in the process of revising, that definition to include oral, rectal, and vaginal contact, as well as penetration. More important, we have come to understand that rape is an act of aggression, not a sexual act performed out of passion or lust. The need to humiliate and overpower, not sexual gratification, is the motivation for the attack.

The act of rape is one of the oldest forms of aggression against women. The Bible relates many tales of rape, as does the folklore of peoples throughout the world. The author Susan Brownmiller has noted that rape has often been considered as "an unfortunate but inevitable by-product of the necessary game called war." Japan, for example, has only recently admitted—and only because it was forced to by public opinion—that during World War II thousands of Korean women were forced into brothels used by the Japanese military. In our own time, we have become aware that many women in war-torn Bosnia-Herzegovina have been raped by Serbian forces. Like rape in general, wartime rape is an act of violence that should be prosecuted as a war crime when it is a deliberate strategy or tactic in the war.

## A BATTLE BETWEEN THE SEXES?

Although the status of American women has risen dramatically during the past century, many men and women remain confused about their sexual and societal roles. Some experts claim that the rising number of violent crimes against women reflects men's intense anger over the political and economic power women appear to be gaining in modern America. As Susan Brownmiller theorized in her landmark book, *Against Our Will: Men, Women and Rape,* "It [rape] is nothing more or less than a conscious process of intimidation by which *all* men keep *all* women in a state of fear." Others see the rise in gender-based violence as stemming from long-held ideas about male aggression ("boys will be boys") and female subjection that are reinforced by a society obsessed with sex in its advertising, music, movies, and television.

# Date Rape

A commonly held misconception about rape is that it involves a surprise attack by a stranger. The truth is that 80 percent of rapes are committed by someone who was known to the survivor—including a husband, a father, an uncle, or other male relative and, increasingly, acquaintances and dates. In fact the term *date rape* has become all too common as more and more women come forward to relate their experiences of being forced to have sex with men whom they were casually dating.

One clue to the persistence and pervasiveness of rape in a supposedly enlightened society can by found in the results of a 1988 survey conducted on a Midwestern college campus. Both young men and women were asked: Is it all right if a male holds a female down and forces her to engage in sexual intercourse (1) if he spends a lot of money on her? (39% of men and 12% of women said yes); (2) if she has had intercourse with others? (39% men and 18% women answered yes); (3) if she says she will have sex and then changes her mind? (54% men and 31% women responded yes). With answers like these it should not be surprising that when 7,000 students were surveyed on 32 campuses, one of eight women said they were raped and one in four women were victims of an attempted rape.

Although rapes can occur anytime of the day or night, according to FBI Uniform Crime Reports it is more likely to happen during the late evening or early morning on a Saturday or Sunday. Rapes occur on poorly lit side streets, in dormitory rooms on college campuses, and in living rooms after casual dates.

(Almost half of all rapes occur in or around the victim's home.) Some rapists use knives, guns, or other weapons to intimidate their victims; others pose a threat by their physical strength alone.

The rape survivor often describes her experience as one in which every aspect of her awareness and being is attuned only to protecting herself and escaping with her life. Depending on her assessment for survival, one woman might physically fight her assailant, while another is unable to resist. If a woman survives a rape, it is proof that she made the right choice; she is therefore considered to be a survivor and not just a victim.

## PREVENTING RAPE

Unfortunately, there is no foolproof way to prevent rape, but there are commonsense steps you can take.

- Take normal precautions against rape: Never walk alone late at night; always make sure your home is secured; never get into a stranger's car; never hitchhike; never allow a stranger to follow you into a building.

- If you live alone, use only your first initial and last name on the mailbox or tenant list.

- Teenage girls, who are particularly vulnerable, should understand that there is safety in numbers and whenever possible should travel in a group. They should be strongly warned against picking up strangers or bringing them back to their homes or dorms.

- If possible, take a self-defense course and learn how to resist an assailant.
- Be aware that any date could turn into a date rape.
- Know the name of every man you date and be somewhat reserved on a first date. (You might offer to pay for half of the date so you don't "owe" him.)
- If you are going to go home with a man you just met (which is never a good idea), tell someone and let the man know that you have done so.
- If any date begins to "cross the line," let him know immediately that you don't approve. Look for an escape route.
- Never allow yourself to be pressured into sexual intercourse. If you feel you are being pressured, extricate yourself from the situation and leave.
- Avoid use of alcohol and drugs.

## The Aftermath: Picking Up the Pieces

The woman who has just survived a rape needs safety, comfort, and crisis intervention. Rape hotlines are available in many communities to give women advice, support, and information about their options in the rape aftermath. Often, however, the survivor feels too afraid, disoriented, ashamed, and defiled by the experience to report it to the authorities or to seek help at a hospital or clinic. Typically the rape survivor only wants to take a hot shower or bath; unfortunately, that also washes off the tangible evidence on her body that sex has taken place. The last thing she may want is an examination of the same intimate parts of her body that were just invaded and abused. And she may well be terrified of further violence from her assailant or be scared that she will receive an unsympathetic response from medical or legal professionals.

However, it is imperative that a rape survivor seek medical care as soon as possible, both to receive emergency medical treatment and to establish evidence that the rape took place. If the survivor goes to the hospital for a post-rape examination, she should be informed that hospitals are generally legally required to report rapes. These rules were established in response to criticism that some survivors—particularly when a wife who accused her husband of rape—were not taken seriously and evidence was not routinely gathered and preserved. (It should be noted that since 1975 more than 30 states have passed laws defining marital rape as a punishable crime.)

When the police are involved, they should make a careful documentation of all injuries. Specimens such as vaginal fluid (which might indicate the presence of semen), foreign bodies, pubic hair, blood, and saliva should be collected as evidence. Photographs of any injuries are especially important because most cuts and bruises are healed by the time the case goes to court.

Once severe injuries are treated, physicians usually offer medication to protect survivors from sexually transmitted diseases that may have been passed by the rapist. Although the reported incidence of gonorrhea following rape is only 3 percent and that of syphilis is 0.1 percent, medical attention can ensure that neither is contracted. If the patient desires, she will be tested for the AIDS virus. (Even if her attacker is caught, the rape survivor is not entitled to know his HIV status, and he cannot be forced to take an AIDS test.) A second test after six months will better determine whether AIDS was contracted. Pregnancy is another problem. Despite a low risk— only about 1 percent of survivors become pregnant following a rape—doctors usually administer medication to prevent conception if requested to do so by the survivor.

The psychological assessment and treatment of the rape survivor is crucial as soon as her medical condition has been stabilized. Indeed, in many ways the physical injuries are easy to treat compared with the longer-lasting emotional scars left by the rape.

## The Psychological Approach

Rape has a profound effect upon a woman's life and her view of the world. Her self-esteem—her image as someone who can operate in the world with some degree of safety and success—may be shattered, and it may be very difficult to put the psychic pieces back together again.

Almost without exception, a survivor blames herself to some extent for the attack. She often bombards herself with accusations: "Why did I take that route home?" "Why did I say yes to the date?" "Why did I wear that dress?" Blaming the victim is part of the rape scenario: In New York one convicted serial rapist said boldly, "Women get raped because of the way they dress." Even friends and family often join in the chorus: "What were you wearing?" "How much did you drink?" "Why did you let him kiss you?" "Why did you go to his room?" The survivor may, in fact, become so obsessed with her role in the rape that she plays the scene over and over again to see if she might have changed the course of events.

When the assailant is someone the survivor knows, which is the case in a large majority of rapes, the guilt and self-blame are compounded and her judgment about all men may be thrown into question. In addition, her ideas about sex and her own sexuality may be distorted by the rape, especially if she, like many women, felt some sexual stimulation at any point during the rape. Becoming sexually active following a rape is difficult for most rape survivors. There are other traumas as well.

## The Rape Trauma Syndrome

Rape survivors appear to pass through several stages of emotional reactions, similar in some ways to those experienced by the grief-stricken. The length of time needed to pass through each stage varies considerably, and many women find themselves returning to different stages during the course of recovery. The common reactions experienced by rape survivors have been described by nursing researchers Burgess and Holwstrum as rape trauma syndrome and are now included by the American Psychiatric Association in descriptions of post-traumatic stress disorder in the diagnostic manual. The physical reactions include pain, nausea, insomnia, changes in sleeping and eating patterns, and hot and cold flashes. Emotional reactions include self-doubt, guilt, mood swings, and anxiety.

Immediately following the rape, the survivor may also feel:

- *Denial.* Numb and uncomprehending, she may deny that the experience happened altogether or rationalize the event away, even if it means convincing herself that she consented.

- *Anger and grief.* After the shock and the denial have worn off, a survivor often moves on to the reaction stage. At this point, the survivor admits to herself that she has in fact been viciously violated and allows herself to react emotionally to the event.

- *Depression.* Faced with a loss of self-esteem, self-confidence ("How did I let that happen to me?"), and for some a loss of independence as they cling to those around them for support and protection, some survivors fall into a long-term depression. Psychotherapy and support groups can be important and helpful at this stage, as long as the therapist or group leader is trained in working with the consequences of trauma on women.

- *The need to take action.* At some point, a woman may choose to transform her lifestyle to protect herself from another attack. Once they have gained some perspective—a process that may take from several days to several years—many survivors become mobilized to take some action relating directly to the rape. For some, this may mean simply telling someone close to them the details of the event; for others it may mean joining a support group or even starting a rape hotline in the community.

- *Acceptance.* A survivor may begin to accept that her sense of safety and view of the world could be permanently altered by experiencing a rape.

## Rape and the Legal System

For many survivors, the process of taking action against the rapist at some stage in the acceptance process can be a powerful healer. By all accounts, however, less than 15 percent of all rapes are reported. Women who are raped by men they know are often particularly reluctant to report it, because they know there is a chance they will not be taken seriously by the criminal justice system. The police investigation is often long and tedious, and the trial does not usually take place until months after the attack. If a woman decides to prosecute, she will need ongoing support from her family as well as from the police, prosecutors, and perhaps her medical team.

Even today, women who are raped feel overwhelmed by a legal system that often places the burden of proof on the victim rather than on the accused. Until only recently an eyewitness was required to prove that a rape had occurred at all. Without question, convicting a rapist in the absence of corroborative evidence such as a serious injury, torn clothes, or blood stains is still difficult.

On the positive side, legislatures in 47 states have passed rape shield laws that limit the so-called loosewoman argument—the defense can no longer focus on a women's sexual past. These laws, which vary by state, protect both the identity and past sexual history of rape survivors while describing the specific "exceptional circumstances" where it will be permitted.

Despite the rape shield laws, during the actual trial the behavior and personal history of the survivor still becomes as much of an issue as the facts surrounding the incident itself. Nevertheless, most women who decide to prosecute ultimately feel more empowered and in control than those who refuse to do so. Psychologically, too, it offers some form of closure to the event.

One survivor who was raped by a former boyfriend clearly understood that it was going to be difficult to prove her charges. As she said, "I don't care if I don't win. When the police arrested him at work, at least I knew I had ruined his day."

Because of the difficulty in winning criminal cases, some women take a different legal route and bring civil charges against the rapist in an attempt to collect damages. Also, a majority of states have passed some form of victim compensation legislation, and the survivor may be reimbursed for medical expenses and lost earnings. The survivor must meet eligibility requirements and may have to cooperate with criminal justice agencies.

## IF YOU ARE IN DANGER OF BEING RAPED

Rape is a crime of violence, in which injury or death may be threatened. Any clues that the rapist gives you about his person, motivations, or weaknesses may be useful in preventing the rape or, if you cannot prevent it, surviving it. Possible strategies are:

- *Make a loud noise.* Many women now routinely

carry a whistle that makes a piercing sound or scream "Police" to attract attention.

- *Run*, but only if there is a safe haven near you. Any attempt to flee that fails may make the situation worse by angering the rapist.

- *Stall* the attacker by speaking calmly and rationally to him. Try not to plead, cry, or otherwise show terror—that may be just the reaction he is hoping to elicit.

- *Urinate or vomit*. If nothing else works, try something that may repulse your attacker. Saying you have a sexually transmitted disease or AIDS may also scare him off, but it may enrage him, too.

- *Fight*. This strategy should be attempted only as a last resort, especially if he has a weapon. However, studies have shown that women who actively resist and who act quickly are more likely to avoid rape than those who are passive or show no resistance. (The optimum time to act is within the first 20 seconds when the body often releases chemicals into the bloodstream that help you to put up a fight.)

- *Do nothing*. Once you feel that you have no chance of avoiding the attack, try not to do anything that will anger the attacker. Some women have made the choice of asking the attacker to use a condom. Although this request could help avoid pregnancy or the spread of a sexually transmitted disease, it has sometimes later been turned against the rape survivor as evidence that she consented.

- *Keep alert.* If you are raped, as difficult as it may be, pay attention to anything that might help you later identify the man: height, skin color, eye color, hair type and color, scars, language and accent, odors, and clothing. When you have the opportunity, write down or even tape facts about the rape.

- *Get help.* As soon as you can, call the police (911). You are the victim of a violent crime and most police now understand this and will help you. Keep in mind that, even if you do call the police, you are not obligated to press charges or take the matter to court. Such decisions can be made at a later date.

- *Collect evidence.* Do not shower, bathe, or douche; if you remove your clothes, put them in a plastic bag and seal it. Although your instinct may be to physically wash away every memory of the event, you will also be destroying evidence that can be used to identify and convict your assailant.

- *Tell someone.* If you do not want to call the police, call a rape crisis counselor—ask the telephone operator to connect you with the nearest center available. It is important that you tell someone—you are less likely to recover if the rape remains your secret.

**For More Information and Help**

National Organization for Victims Assistance
1757 Park Road N.W.
Washington, DC 20010
202-232-6682

Violence Against Women Act Task Force
NOW Legal Defense and Education Task Force
99 Hudson Street
New York, NY 10013
212-925-6635
Washington, D.C., office: 202-544-4470

# CHILDHOOD SEXUAL ABUSE

A random survey of 769 college students indicated that 20 percent of girls and 9 percent of boys reported they had been sexually abused before they were 18. Other sources estimate that the number could be as high as one in every four girls and one in every seven boys.

The sexual abuse may take many forms, including sexually suggestive language, prolonged kissing and petting, vaginal and/or anal intercourse, and oral sex. It can be one or two incidents in a short period of time or continue over several years. Young girls are often abused by men they know: fathers, stepfathers, grandfathers, uncles, brothers, cousins, their mothers' or sisters' boyfriends. (A small percentage of children are abused by their mothers.) The abuser is typically someone who is welcomed into the victim's home. Some children are abused by people they come in contact with on a regular basis and whom they have been taught by their parents to trust, such as neighbors, coaches, clergymen, teachers, baby-sitters, doctors, dentists, and camp counselors.

A sexual relationship with an adult is, by its very nature, one over which the child has no control;

because it often occurs within the family context or with a trusted family friend or teacher, the child may assume there is implied parental approval. Incest—sex with a member of one's family—and sexual abuse in general are never the child's fault. The law correctly insists that sexual abuse is always the fault of the adult. In father-daughter incest, for example, it is the father who chooses the relationship. Even if the rationale is that the daughter "asked for it," it is the adult's responsibility to say no.

## SIGNS OF SEXUAL ABUSE

Sexual abuse is often perpetrated without physical force or battery, so the child may not show overt signs of abuse. For this reason, it is important to be aware of the subtle clues that may signal a child's distress. Physical signs include:

- lacerations, irritation, pain, or injury to the genital area;
- discharge from the genital area;
- pregnancy;
- a sexually transmitted disease;
- difficulty with urination.

Behavioral indications include:

- one child being treated in a significantly different way from other children in the family;
- aggressive, hostile, or disruptive behavior toward adults;
- provocative behavior (including flirting);

- sudden regressive behavior such as acting child-ish and crying;
- inability to make friends.

Sometimes the clues come directly from the child; the adult needs to hear between the lines. Be suspicious if a child says, "He fooled around with me," "I don't like to be alone with...," or "I'm afraid to go home." These signs are now taught to teachers, day-care workers, and other adults who come in regular contact with children. Most states have laws that require professionals who work with children to report suspected child abuse to a responsible agency.

**To Report Abuse**

National Child Abuse Hotline
1-800-422-4453

Parents Anonymous
1-800-423-0353

**For More Information and Help**

National Committee for Prevention of Child Abuse
332 South Michigan Avenue
Chicago, IL 60604
312-663-3520

# The Aftermath of Child Abuse

The reactions of the child vary widely depending on the age of the child; her stage of development; the amount of fear, physical violence, and pain that the child experiences; the frequency and length of time over which the abuse occurs; and the reaction of nonabusing adults.

Because the experience of sexual abuse runs so counter to a child's need to love and relate to the adults in her life, it is frequently dissociated from the child's consciousness. Often the child visualizes herself out of her body, thereby losing perceptions, feelings, and whole blocks of memory. (An extreme form of dissociation may result in a child developing multiple personalities.) Although the psychological mechanisms of dissociation and denial of the experience help the child survive at the time of abuse, they often play havoc in her later life. The suppressed experience often manifests itself in fear, repression of emotions, and the inability to form lasting, healthy relationships.

Survivors of incest and sexual abuse know that the emotional and physical scars often last for a lifetime. The victim often blames herself long after the abuse has ended—for not saying no, for not fighting back, for not telling anyone about the abuse, for having trusted the abuser.

Some survivors feel the need to confront their abuser and to hear the person admit that the events actually took place. Those who decide to prosecute often face the same kind of difficulty faced by battered or raped women. The legal and medical professions are, however, becoming more sensitive in recognizing, treating, and taking action against child abuse.

# DOMESTIC BATTERY

More than two million women a year are officially identified as abuse survivors. Since this number reflects just the reported cases, the true scope of the problem can only be estimated. It is thought by some that an astounding 30 to 40 percent of the injuries that cause adult women to go to hospital emergency rooms have been inflicted by batterers. Most women who are battered by their husbands or lovers will suffer repeated injuries over several months and even years. Some will even die at the hands of their batterers. Battery first may take the form of implied threats ("If you ever talk to me that way again, I won't be responsible for the outcome") and then escalate to physical violence: shoving, punching, kicking, biting, scalding, choking, and marital rape. Most abusive injuries are inflicted on the head, neck, chest, abdomen, and breasts. Injuries may also occur on the arms, which are used to deflect blows. Physicians treating abused women report every kind of injury imaginable, from broken ribs to detached retinas to mutilated sexual organs. In addition to physical abuse, women may find themselves the victims of emotional abuse; their husbands or lovers so verbally humiliate and abase them that nothing is left of their self-esteem or self-confidence. Quite often, emotional abuse escalates into physical violence.

Like rape, battery has been around since the beginning of time. Popular culture abounds with examples of battery, from the *Honeymooners* TV show (bus driver Ralph Kramden regularly threatened to send Alice "to the moon") to the Rolling Stones song "Under My Thumb." Rappers, too, regularly sing about "slapping my bitch."

The roots of the battery syndrome are as deep as those from which rape grows, and in many ways the patterns are similar. Battery is a pattern of behavior that results in a man establishing power over a woman through fear and intimidation. Battery usually occurs when men believe they are entitled to control their partners, and it continues because battered women usually end up believing it too. That is why it is believed to be such an unreported epidemic.

Like rapists, batterers come in all shapes, sizes, and ethnic backgrounds. But they do share several common characteristics: they are generally insecure, frustrated, jealous, possessive, and often display a Jekyll-and-Hyde personality, alternating periods of abuse with periods of affection. Almost all abusive husbands come from homes in which there was physical abuse between their fathers and mothers, and many battered wives also witnessed physical and emotional battery as they grew up. Because parents serve as powerful role models, children learn that violence is a useful and effective way to bring about desired behavior. The male child learns from watching his mother's reaction that she is afraid of the father, and he may apply this knowledge in adulthood by using violence or the threat of violence to achieve his own goals. A female child exposed to battery will learn passivity at all costs and, perhaps, that violence is a man's natural right. The pattern of abuse is a vicious circle that is hard to break.

## The Abusive Relationship

Although there is a small percentage of women for whom violence is so much a part of the fabric of their lives that they enter a relationship knowing that there may be violence, most relationships are loving at the beginning. Indeed, for most women, violence inflicted by their mates comes as a surprise and at first may seem to be an aberration. However, a pattern emerges in which anger and tension build within the male partner until he explodes in a violent episode. After his rage is spent, he usually expresses deep remorse and promises that he will never do it again. Such a cycle is repeated over and over again until the woman no longer believes in herself or in the man to whom she is committed.

These relationships often reach a special intensity. The perpetrator of the violence is very attuned to the woman's every action, to her presence or absence, and to whether or not she is attending to his needs. Each episode of violence gives the man more coercive power over his victim, and as it continues, he may limit her access to food, sleep, and medical care. (He may even hide her car keys.) Indeed, isolation is a powerful weapon in the batterer's arsenal: a battering husband usually stops his victim from communicating with friends or relatives and swears her to secrecy, even threatening to kill her if she tells anyone about the violence.

In turn, the battered woman becomes hypersensitive to the man in her life as he demands more and more of her attention. She often feels forced to obey his commands about her housekeeping, her meal preparation, and her behavior toward others. Freedom for the battered woman ends when her husband comes home, and it is replaced with submissive, often fearful, behavior linked to the perpetrator's moods and desires. Because inadvertent actions may bring on his violence, battered women live in a constant state of terror. (Anything can tip the scale toward violence, but alcohol seems to be a trigger.) If children are part of the family, they, too, become involved in the pattern of fear and violence.

Why do women stay in violent relationships? Often out of terror because of their partners' threats to kill them or take their children away. The less educated and able to earn money a woman is, the more likely she is to stay in the relationship. Although the role of women in the workplace is changing, women still face fewer job opportunities and usually earn considerably less than men. If the woman has children, the challenge is compounded. She can't help but be aware that even a court award of child support is no guarantee of economic stability. And there is still strong societal pressure to "stand by your man." The victim is strongly (if figuratively) tied to her batterer—she is bound by a combination of threats, intimidation, manipulation, control, and coercion.

Battered women often feel too ashamed and full of self-blame and hatred to admit that they've let themselves be hit over and over again. Many women are so numb from repeated abuse and injury that they are barely able to function, and they sleepwalk through their lives. Battered women typically experience extreme anxiety and depression; in fact, 26 percent of all women who attempt suicide are survivors of violence. Battered women are 16 times as likely to abuse alcohol as the average adult woman, and many abuse drugs. Trapped by circumstances that seem to be beyond their control, battered women often suffer through years of physical and emotional torture at the hands of their mates before they reach out for help.

*Myth:* "He can't live without me."
*Truth:* You can't live with him.

*Myth:* "The kids need a father."
*Truth:* Kids do not need a father who is likely to beat them as well.

*Myth:* "It will get better."
*Truth:* It only gets worse.

*Myth:* "He'll kill me if I go."
*Truth:* He may well kill you if you stay.

## Getting Out, Getting Help

Although doctors and nurses are often in a good position to recognize abuse and to intervene, research has shown that they often fail to report such incidents to the police or to explore the reason for the violence with the patient. Doctors are increasingly able to identify symptoms and then to help a battered woman recognize the serious, often life-threatening, circumstances in which she finds herself. Keeping the woman's safety and the safety of her children in mind, the physician may help her remove herself from the abusive situation.

Women who are beaten are twice as likely to be beaten when they are pregnant. Pregnant abused women suffer from emotional stress, have less prenatal care, often don't follow nutritional guidelines, and

## PORTRAIT OF AN ABUSER

What kind of person would physically and emotionally abuse his wife? Researchers are still searching for answers, but studies have pointed out the following characteristics:

- Abusers have a need to control the environment around them, especially the people who are closest to them. Beating up their wives periodically is one way to ensure compliance.

- Men who have been brought up in a violent home are most likely to abuse their female partners. Other risk factors are unemployment, less education, and drug and alcohol use. One should not forget, however, that many well-educated professional men—doctors, lawyers, business executives—also beat their partners.

- Many abusers are dependent on their wives and jealous of them. Fearing abandonment, they minimize the attacks and blame the victim for any violence inflicted on her.

Unfortunately, abusive men often resist treatment. Court-ordered batterers' education and treatment groups (which address the battering as a criminal means to power and control) have had reasonable success. A few men do come to such groups voluntarily. Conventional models of couples or family therapy are absolutely contraindicated where one member of the couple is committing criminal assaults on the other. Most important, men must be confronted with the results of their battery and learn that if they don't change their behavior, they will go to jail.

are more likely to abuse alcohol and drugs. Few studies have examined the effects of abuse on pregnant women, but it appears that physical abuse may cause injuries or aggravate chronic illnesses that lead to decreased fetal growth or premature birth.

When a battered woman seeks psychological help, it is critical that the therapist understand that her symptoms, no matter how severe, are a product of her terror, isolation, and inability to escape her situation and in most cases are not indicative of a long-term psychological disorder. The therapist cannot get an accurate view of the underlying problems until the source of terror is removed. The impact of many psychological diagnoses is to create or reinforce the idea that the problem of violence is her fault. Sometimes tranquilizers or antidepressants are prescribed to help a battered woman to function, but it is important for both physician and patient to keep medications to a minimum. If she is oversedated, she may not recognize danger or act on it in time to save herself or her children.

A particularly dangerous time for the battered woman is when she is planning, carrying out, or has recently achieved her escape. Most women who die at the hands of their abuser are killed at this time. It is also after the decision has been made to leave that a desperate woman may turn on the perpetrator during an attack and kill him. Most women who kill their abusers see no possibility of escape. Women who kill their batterers often report that those to whom they turned in the legal or medical professions could not or did not help.

# IF YOU ARE BATTERED

- If your husband or lover hits you, try to defend yourself, paying particular attention to protecting your stomach and head.

- Call for help, scream, and if you can get away, run.

- Fight back only if you judge that it won't make him hurt you more. Retaliating with violence tends to cause escalation of the violence.

- Document the abuse by taking pictures or telling someone—a friend, a neighbor, or the police (call 911). If you do call the police, get a copy of the police report.

- Threatening to divorce or leave your partner *may* interrupt the violence.

- A personal safety plan is essential. A counselor or advocate from a domestic violence program may help you work one out. Plan possible destinations in an emergency with friends, relatives, or a shelter. Keep the money necessary to get there, and have a survival fund for yourself. Plan a means of transportation. Have some clothes and personal essentials packed or at a safe location. Plan for your children also.

**For More Information**

202-232-6682 is a national 24-hour hotline.

National Coalition Against Domestic Violence
P.O. Box 18749
Denver, CO 80218-0749
303-839-1852

National Clearinghouse for the Defense
  of Battered Women
137 S. 9th Street
Philadelphia, PA
215-351-0010


## Life After Battery

Since domestic violence emerged as a topic of dis-
cussion in the late 1970s, most communities across
the country have opened hotlines and shelters to battered women. Some medical facilities have a social
worker available. It is critical for a battered woman to
find whatever resources and support are available in
her community.

Shelters can be a lifesaver, providing a woman
and her children with a safe haven for an average stay
of about four to six weeks. (About half of the children
who are admitted to women's shelters have also been
abused.) A shelter is a place where a woman can
begin to heal her emotional and physical wounds
while slowly regaining her self-confidence and ability to function. She can also learn about her legal
options in terms of divorce, child support, and, if she
wishes, criminal prosecution of her abuser.

In many states police and prosecutory practices
are rapidly improving. Police are being trained to be
more sensitive and many cities now have mandatory
arrest policies for a batterer. In many cities prosecutors will pursue the case whether or not the victim
presses charges.

Testimony from battered women in court cases
and in interviews emphasizes that the first step to

recovery is to admit that the abuse exists as a real problem. The next step is to stop hoping that the problem will go away. Once an abused woman recognizes that she (and her children) have every right to feel safe in her home, she is on her way to finding the self-confidence she needs to rebuild her life. After a woman leaves the abusive situation behind her, she is often able to have healthier subsequent relationships.

## Moving Toward Solutions

In recent years, the problem of violence against girls and women has been viewed as a public health crisis. We can all take small steps by walking with other women in "Take Back the Night" rallies, volunteering in shelters, and reporting child abuse if we suspect it. We can help break the cycle of violence by breaking the silence—by sharing our own experiences.

# PART IV

# Substance Abuse in Women

Roselyn Payne Epps, M.D., M.P.H., M.A., F.A.A.P., and Anne Geller, M.D.

Over the centuries, drugs have been used for rituals, for pain relief, for social bonding, and to help people function day to day. When used properly, some drugs are not harmful. If abused, however, mind-altering drugs can pose serious health risks, cause dependency, and interfere with work and relationships. Women should be aware of the risks of drugs. They can then make informed choices about using them and know when to seek help at the first signs of trouble.

Statistically, women are less likely than men to abuse drugs, but substance use among women is increasing at an alarming rate. Cigarette smoking, for example, has decreased overall but has increased among women aged 16–22, who are more likely than their male counterparts to smoke. Estimates indicate that of the 15.1 million Americans who abuse alcohol or are alcohol-dependent, 4.6 million are women. This means that roughly one third of alcoholics are women.

Women are prone to special problems linked with drug use. Although they may drink less than men, the health impact on women is greater. They are more subject to alcohol-related liver disease, experience menstrual disorders associated with alcohol use, and are more likely to become victims of aggressive acts when under the influence of alcohol. Over twice as many women as men are admitted to emergency rooms as a result of the overuse of tranquilizers. More than 80 percent of cases of acquired immune deficiency syndrome (AIDS) in women are associated with intravenous drug use. And the use of cigarettes, alcohol, and other drugs during pregnancy can cause serious harm to the fetus, especially in the first weeks of gestation, when a woman may not know she is pregnant.

# HOW DRUGS AFFECT THE MIND AND BODY

Messages are sent from the body to the brain by means of electrical signals that are conveyed to the nerve cells in the brain through neurotransmitters. Any substance that interferes with these neuro-transmitters, such as mood-altering drugs, can short-circuit these messages. Different drugs have different effects, but they all affect brain chemistry. Even small changes can greatly affect one's mood.

There are four types of mind-altering drugs: sedatives, narcotics, stimulants, and hallucinogens (see Table 4.1). All have the potential for psychological dependence and physical addiction. Because these drugs affect the part of the brain responsible for pleasure, euphoria, or pain relief, they can easily lead to abuse. The risk increases with the strength of the drug, the amount, the speed with which it reaches the brain, and how often it is taken. In order of increasing risk, drugs can be taken by mouth, by sniffing or snorting, by smoking, and by injecting into a vein.

The effects of drugs vary with the individual. Men seem to process alcohol in their bodies faster than women, for example. The very young and the very old are more intolerant of drugs. Weight is also a factor; those who weigh less are affected more. Many drug takers use more than one substance at a time—either an illegal drug, alcohol, or tobacco. Older women especially are not only more susceptible to

## TABLE 4.1. TYPES OF MIND-ALTERING DRUGS

| Sedatives | Narcotics | Stimulants | Hallucinogens |
|-----------|-----------|------------|---------------|
| *Drugs in Everyday Products* | | | |
| | | Alcohol | |
| | | Caffeine | |
| | | Nicotine | |
| | | | |
| *Prescription Drugs* | | | |
| SLEEPING PILLS | Codeine | Benzedrine | |
| Amytal | Darvon | Control | |
| Dalmane | Demerol | Dexedrine | |
| Doriden | Dilaudid | Dexatrim | |
| Halcion | Lomotil | Methedrine | |
| Nembutal | Methadone | Preludin | |
| Placidyl | Morphine | Ritalin | |
| Quaalude | Percodan | Tennate | |
| Seconal | Talwin | | |
| TRANQUILIZERS | | | |
| Ativan | | | |
| Librium | | | |

| Sedatives | Narcotics | Stimulants | Hallucinogens |
|---|---|---|---|
| Miltown | | | Marijuana (grass, pot, weed) |
| Serax | | | Hash |
| Tranxene | | | LSD (acid, cube, D) |
| Valium | | | PCP (angel dust, hog, peace pill) |
| *Street Drugs* | | | |
| Blues | Heroin (skag, horse, junk, stuff) | Bennies | |
| Downs | | Cocaine (crack, snow, flake, coke) | |
| Goofballs | Methadone (dollies) | Crystal | |
| Nembies | Darvon (pinks and greens) | Dexies | |
| Red devils | | Hearts | |
| Yellowjackets | | Speed | |

alcohol but also often take multiple medications that can interact with even small amounts of alcohol to produce a harmful reaction.

# WHO IS AT RISK?

Women who are at higher risk for substance abuse include those with the following history:

- Biologic daughter of an alcohol- or drug-abusing parent
- Spouse of an alcoholic or drug abuser
- Women who have recently experienced traumatic life events, such as:

  Divorce or separation

  Death of spouse or significant other

  Job loss

  Retirement

  Rape or sexual abuse

  Witnessed a traumatic event
- Women with a physical handicap or disability
- Health care professionals
- Women who have a psychiatric disorder (depression, psychosis, anxiety, hyperactivity)

There are both physical and psychological signs of drug abuse. Some physical signs include tremors, slurred speech, irregular heartbeat, cough and runny nose, and nervous mannerisms. Psychological problems can include memory loss, panic, paranoia, unexplained mood swings, and personality changes. Vague complaints such as fatigue, insomnia, headaches, sexual problems, and loss of appetite can be early red flags that a person may have a drug problem.

# TYPES OF DRUGS AND THEIR EFFECTS

## Tobacco

Cigarette smoking is the single most preventable cause of disease and death in the United States. The statistics are grim:

- The average cigarette smoker shortens her life by 5–8 years.

- One of every six deaths in the United States is related to smoking.

- Cigarette smoking now contributes to 30 percent of all cancer deaths.

- Smoking is responsible for over half of the deaths from cardiovascular disease in women less than 65 years old.

- Smoking is linked to various types of cancer, chronic lung disease, and reproductive problems.

Despite these serious health risks, 26 percent of reproductive-age women (18–44 years old) smoke an average of 18 cigarettes per day. Smoking is also on the rise among young women; the number of smokers aged 12–18 years has doubled in the past 10 years. More teenage girls than boys now smoke. This trend toward early initiation of smoking behavior is ominous because many of the health risks associated with smoking increase both with earlier onset and duration of the smoking.

The number of women smokers is almost the same as the number of male smokers, because more men than women have stopped smoking. But

---

## ADDICTIVE PERSONALITY TRAITS

Certain personality traits appear to be linked to drug abuse:

- Impulsiveness
- Difficulty in delaying gratification
- Sensation-seeking
- Rebelliousness
- Weak commitment to social goals
- Sense of alienation
- Low tolerance for stress

Other characteristics (may appear in combination with above):

- Low self-esteem
- Vulnerability to anxiety and depression
- History of conflicting parental expectations

women are as susceptible as men to the harmful effects of tobacco. In addition, smoking during pregnancy poses special concerns to a woman and her fetus.

## What Is in a Cigarette?

Cigarette smoking became popular among women after 1940 as more and more women entered the work force. During 1953–54, there was a decline in the number of cigarettes smoked as reports began to emerge linking cigarette smoking and lung cancer. The Surgeon General has identified ways in which smoking cigarettes poses risks for lung cancer and other lung disorders. The Surgeon General's 1988 report warned that nicotine, a main ingredient in cigarettes, is as addictive as heroin and cocaine. Smoking, the report stated, must be viewed as a life-threatening addiction and not merely an unhealthy habit. In 1992, the Environmental Protection Agency (EPA) classified tobacco smoke as a class A carcinogen, placing it in the same category of cancer-causing agents as asbestos and benzene.

These early warnings led to the increased use of filter cigarettes and brands with less tar and nicotine. Lower tar and nicotine cigarettes are not the answer, however. The reported amounts of these harmful substances do not necessarily represent the smoker's actual intake. Also, evidence is mounting that individuals who switch to these brands inhale more deeply, smoke a greater proportion of cigarettes and, in some cases, smoke more. Many conventional filter cigarettes may, in fact, deliver more carbon monoxide than nonfilter cigarettes. Even the lowest yield cigarettes present health hazards that are very much higher than not smoking at all.

More than 4,000 chemicals have been identified in tobacco smoke, including carbon monoxide, oxides of nitrogen, ammonia, polycyclic aromatic hydrocarbons, hydrogen cyanide, vinyl chloride, and

## TABLE 4.2.   WOMEN SMOKERS

| Characteristic | 1992 % |
|---|---|
| Race/Ethnicity | |
| White | 25.9 |
| African American | 24.1 |
| Hispanic | 18.0 |
| American Indian/Alaskan Native | 39.8 |
| Asian/Pacific Islander | 4.0 |
| Education level (yrs) | |
| <12 | 27.5 |
| 12 | 28.2 |
| 13–15 | 23.1 |
| 16 | 14.6 |
| Age group (yrs) | |
| 18–24 | 24.9 |
| 25–44 | 28.8 |
| 45–64 | 26.1 |
| ≥65 | 12.4 |
| Socioeconomic status | |
| Above poverty level | 23.8 |
| Below poverty level | 31.7 |
| Unknown | 22.1 |
| Total | 24.6 |

nicotine. Many of these substances are known carcinogens.

Nicotine is the addictive substance in cigarettes. Nicotine affects all major organs and systems in the body, including the nervous system, voluntary muscles, stomach, intestines, heart, brain, and oral cavity. Nicotine is distributed throughout the body and processed by several organs, including the liver. Eventually, it is cleared through the kidneys.

Nicotine is an addictive substance that reinforces and strengthens the desire to smoke. Nicotine stimulates the release of the brain's opiates, the endorphins, which have a number of effects on the brain. Smoking can alter brain chemicals to promote feelings of reward and well-being, reduce anxiety, and reduce hunger. For these reasons, nicotine creates a psychological as well as a physical dependence.

## IMPACT OF SMOKING ON WOMEN

The lack of large-scale studies that focus specifically on female populations makes it difficult to fully assess the impact of smoking on women. However, women show the same responses to cigarette smoking as men. Depending on the number of cigarettes smoked per day, the age of beginning cigarette smoking, and the amount of inhalation, women have death rates similar to men.

In general, women who are smokers experience more illness and chronic conditions than women who have never smoked. According to the American Cancer Society, women who smoke heavily have nearly three times more bronchitis and emphysema, 75 percent more chronic sinusitis, and 50 percent more peptic ulcers than nonsmokers. The incidence of illness, such as influenza, for women smokers is 20 percent higher for women who smoke than for those who don't. Currently employed women smokers report more days lost from work due to illness and injury than working women who do not smoke. In addition, women under 65 years of age who smoke have more limited physical activity than those who have never smoked. More than that, women smokers show an increased rate of heart attacks, cancer, oral diseases, and lung conditions.

## Cardiovascular Disease

Coronary heart disease, including heart attacks, is the major cause of death among women in the United States. In general, cigarette smoking doubles the risk: Carbon monoxide slows the transfer of oxygen from the blood to the body. Nicotine increases the heart rate by 15–25 beats per minute, and blood pressure goes up by 15–25 points. When combined with high blood pressure and high blood cholesterol, smoking multiplies the risk of having a heart attack.

Women smokers who also use oral contraceptives are 10 times more at risk for having a heart attack. Additionally, smoking increases the risk for hypertension and brain hemorrhage.

# Cancer

There has been a rapid increase in the number of lung cancer deaths among women. Women who are heavy smokers are 24 times more likely to develop lung cancer than those who have never smoked, and lung cancer is now the leading cause of cancer deaths in women, exceeding even breast cancer.

The warning signals of lung cancer are:

- A cough that won't go away
- Sputum (secretion coughed up from the lungs) streaked with blood
- Chest pain
- Recurring attacks of pneumonia or bronchitis

Lung cancer is often discovered in advanced stages of the disease, when it is difficult to treat and when it is too late to be cured by surgery. Only 13 percent of lung cancer patients live 5 or more years after it is diagnosed (see box on "The Problem of Passive Smoking").

Cigarette smoking also is linked with cancer of the larynx, the mouth, the esophagus, and the pancreas. Heavy alcohol intake combined with cigarette smoking increases the risk of oral, laryngeal, and esophageal cancer. In women, smoking is associated with cancer of the cervix.

# Oral Cavity Diseases

Tobacco use is a prime cause of oral diseases, including cancer and other serious conditions. Smoking also increases dental treatment management risks and problems. Those who use tobacco show slower healing of wounds, and periodontal disease treatment may be negatively affected by smoking.

## Lung Disease

There is a rising death rate due to chronic obstructive pulmonary disease (COPD) among women who smoke. The prevalence of chronic bronchitis varies directly with the number of cigarettes smoked per

---

### THE PROBLEM OF PASSIVE SMOKING

Cigarette smokers are not the only ones to suffer from cigarette smoke. Tobacco smoke in the environment, also called passive, secondhand, or environmental smoke, is harmful to anyone around the smoker. In fact, studies have shown that environmental tobacco smoke is a cause of lung cancer in humans, responsible for about 3,000 lung cancer deaths annually in the United States. Women who live or work with smokers are especially at risk.

Exposure to tobacco smoke also causes tissue irritation. The main effects are in the eyes and mucous membranes of the nose, throat, and lower respiratory system. Children who are exposed to passive smoke are more likely to suffer from respiratory illness, severe asthma, and middle ear problems.

day. A close relationship also exists between cigarette smoking and chronic cough and sputum production, which increases with the number of cigarettes smoked.

Smoking also causes emphysema, a progressive disease that destroys the elasticity of the lungs and makes it difficult to breathe. Almost 80 percent of people with emphysema smoke or once smoked.

# SMOKING AND REPRODUCTION

Studies in women and men suggest that cigarette smoking may impair fertility. In women, substantial data demonstrate that smoking lowers the age of menopause. The average age of menopause in non-smokers is 50; among women smoking one half pack a day, it is 49; in those smoking one or more packs a day, 48. Evidence suggests that the earlier menopause of smokers is not related to weight differences between smokers and nonsmokers but rather is a direct result of some component of cigarette smoke. Smoking also increases the risk of osteoporosis, a condition that causes the bones to become brittle and break, in postmenopausal women.

## Smoking During Pregnancy

Smoking during pregnancy increases the risk of miscarriage, stillbirth, preterm delivery, and low birth weight. When a pregnant woman smokes she risks her own health and that of her baby, before, during, and after birth.

Babies born to women who smoke during pregnancy weigh, on the average, 7 ounces less than babies born to nonsmoking women. The relation between smoking by the mother and lower birth weight is separate from other factors that can influence birth weight, including race, number of previous births, maternal weight, socioeconomic status, sex of the child, and length of the pregnancy. If a woman gives up smoking early in her pregnancy, her risk of having a low-birthweight baby approaches that of a nonsmoker.

The risk of spontaneous abortion, fetal death, and neonatal death increases directly with levels of maternal smoking during pregnancy. Increasing levels of smoking result in a significant increase in the risk of early separation of the placenta, which connects the mother and fetus, and rupture of the membranes that surround the fetus and contain the amniotic fluid. There is also a higher risk of complications during pregnancy for women who smoke.

Babies of smokers seem to be more susceptible to diseases. Sudden infant death syndrome (SIDS) occurs $2^1/_2$ times more often among babies of smoking mothers.

## HOW TO QUIT SMOKING

The benefits of not smoking start within days of quitting. As the carbon monoxide level in your blood decreases, the oxygen level increases. The heartbeat slows to normal, and the lungs begin to clear and heal.

After 1 or 2 years of not smoking, your risk of a heart attack drops sharply and gradually returns to normal after about 10 years. The risk of cancer is gradually reduced, coming close to that of nonsmokers after 10–15 years. In addition to health benefits, quitting smoking also creates a healthy environment for others in the household. Spouses of nonsmokers have half the lung cancer risk of spouses living with smokers, and infants are less apt to experience respiratory and ear problems.

Despite all the incentives, smoking is not easy to give up. But every year more than 3 million Americans quit smoking. Nearly half of all adults who ever smoked have quit for life.

## The Steps to Smoking Cessation

First, decide to quit. Try to avoid negative thoughts about how difficult it might be (see "Gradual Ways to Quit Smoking"). Some ideas that will help are:

- List all the reasons you want to quit and review the reasons every day.
- Begin to condition yourself physically: Exercise, drink more fluids, get plenty of rest, and avoid fatigue.
- Set a target date for quitting—perhaps your birthday, your anniversary, or some other day of personal significance.
- On the day you quit, throw away all your cigarettes and matches, and hide your ashtrays and lighter.

- Visit the dentist to get your teeth cleaned of the cigarette stains.
- Ask your family and friends to help you over the rough spots.

The first few days after quitting, spend as much free time as possible in places where smoking isn't allowed. Develop a clean, fresh, nonsmoking environment around yourself at work and at home.

Many people who are considering quitting, especially women, are concerned about gaining weight. Quitting doesn't necessarily result in weight gain, however. About one third of ex-smokers gain weight, but another one third actually lose a few pounds. When ex-smokers gain weight, it is usually because they eat more. On average, expect to gain anywhere from 5 to 20 pounds. Your weight gain can be minimal if you eat low-fat foods and exercise.

Many smokers have withdrawal symptoms when they quit. Symptoms usually occur within 24 hours of stopping smoking: Some of the more common symptoms are lack of concentration, anxiety, irritability, insomnia, fatigue, constipation, and hunger. These are signs that the body is recovering from smoking and clearing itself of nicotine, a powerful addictive chemical. Be patient. Most of the nicotine is gone from the body in 2–3 days and withdrawal symptoms usually end within 2–4 weeks. The urge to smoke will last longer, however.

Some people find it easier to quit by using a nicotine patch or nicotine gum. These forms of nicotine replacement deliver small doses of the drug to the body in an attempt to help smokers wean themselves off cigarettes. Although nicotine replacements may relieve the symptoms of withdrawal, they may not completely relieve the craving for cigarettes.

Both the gum and the patch are considered medications and must be prescribed by a physician or dentist. The dose varies with the individual's previous level of smoking. Do not continue smoking after starting the medication. Nicotine replacement should not be used by pregnant or breastfeeding women, or by people with certain heart conditions or health problems.

The unpleasant aftereffects of quitting are only temporary. They signal the beginning of a healthier life. The benefits of giving up cigarettes far outweigh the drawbacks.

## The Relapse Factor

Most relapses occur in the first week after quitting, when withdrawal symptoms are strongest and your body is still dependent on nicotine. Gird yourself against the urge to resume smoking by calling on all your willpower, family, and friends to get you through this critical period. Other relapses occur during the first 3 months after quitting, when certain stressful situations may have you reaching automatically for a cigarette—your old pathway to relaxation. Keep alert to these relapse potentials, and avoid them.

If the urge to smoke is overwhelming, remind yourself that you've quit and you're now a nonsmoker. Then analyze your sudden urge to smoke. Ask yourself these questions:

- Where was I when I got the urge?

## GRADUAL WAYS TO QUIT SMOKING

Many people go cold turkey when they throw away their cigarettes—it's a tried and true method that might work for you. If you prefer a more gradual approach, try these steps:

- *Switch brands.* Try a brand that you find distasteful, or change to a brand that's low in tar and nicotine a few weeks before your target date for quitting. Don't smoke more cigarettes, however, or inhale more often or more deeply.

- *Cut down on the number of cigarettes you smoke.* Smoke only half of each cigarette, or decide that you'll smoke only during particular times of the day. Or decide beforehand how many cigarettes you'll smoke during the day. There's no substitute for quitting, however. If you're down to five or six cigarettes a day, quit.

- *Think before you light up.* Smoke only those cigarettes you really want. Don't smoke only out of habit. Make yourself aware of each cigarette you smoke—put the pack in an unfamiliar location or look in the mirror each time you light up. You may decide you don't need it.

- *Make smoking inconvenient.* Stop buying cigarettes by the carton. Wait until one pack is empty before buying another. Don't carry cigarettes with you at home or at work. Make it tough to get one.

- What was I doing at the time?
- Whom was I with?
- What was I thinking?

Typical triggers to smoking include working under pressure, feeling blue, finishing a meal, watching television, having a drink, and watching someone else smoke. Anticipate these triggers and prepare to avoid them. Find activities that make smoking difficult. Exercise. Avoid places where smoking is permitted. Reduce your consumption of alcohol, which often stimulates the desire to smoke. And reward yourself for not smoking—treat yourself to a concert, a movie, or a new dress.

# ALCOHOL

Alcohol has long been an integral part of most societies, although it is a custom that has not always included women. As women left the home and increasingly entered the work force, they also faced decisions about what constitutes an acceptable level of drinking. The line between alcohol use, or social drinking, and abuse may be hard to draw. In general, alcohol use is light to moderate drinking—one or two drinks at different times. Abuse is drinking in large amounts or in binges.

The number of women in the United States who drink alcohol has increased significantly over the past 40 years. About 60 percent of adult women in the United States drink, and nearly half drink once a week or more.

According to one survey, 3.5 million American women are using alcohol inappropriately and may be classified as suffering from alcoholism. Young women (ages 21–34) report the highest rates of specific drinking-related problems. About 16 percent of young, employed women are heavy drinkers, consuming 3–5 drinks per day. Women ages 35–49 have the highest rates of chronic alcohol problems. It is also estimated that 10–15 percent of the elderly women in this country abuse alcohol, many of whom developed the problem after age 60.

Drinking varies among women of different racial or ethnic backgrounds. African American women are less likely to drink than white women. Hispanic women drink infrequently, less than African American or white women, although this may change as they enter new social and work arenas. Marital status also influences drinking habits. Single, divorced, or separated women are more likely to drink heavily and experience alcohol-related problems than women who are married or widowed. Unmarried women who are living with partners are most likely to develop drinking problems. Alcoholism tends to run in families, and alcoholics often marry other alcoholics. (See Fig. 4.1)

A drinking problem can develop over time. For some women, alcohol problems take 10–20 years to develop; in others such problems occur in a matter of months. Abuse can also arise as the result of a life crisis, such as the loss of a loved one, or stress imposed by marriage and family problems, or financial difficulties. Alcohol can cause problems when used as a means of combating low self-esteem or to overcome loneliness or shyness. Women may become addicted

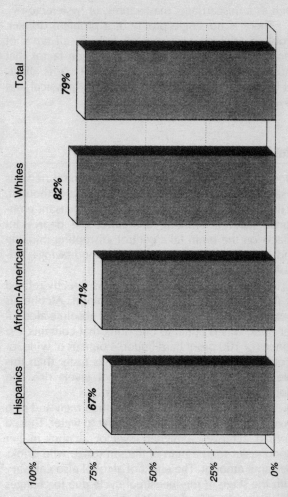

**Figure 4.1.** U.S. Women Who Have Used Alcohol (%, 1992).

to alcohol to help them deal with a physical loss, such as a miscarriage, mastectomy, or hysterectomy.

There is no single profile of a problem drinker. Problem drinking occurs at all ages, in all types of people. Likewise, there is no one single factor that causes problems with alcohol. Alcohol use is affected by a variety of factors, including the physical and psychological effects of dependency.

## The Effects of Alcohol

Alcohol is a drug that depresses the central nervous system. The initial effect is to stimulate thought, action, and sociability, or to induce a pleasant emotional state. If drinking continues, the depressant effects on the brain take control, disrupting thinking and coordination and resulting in mood swings, irritability, and depression.

The strength of alcohol's effect is directly related to the amount of alcohol in the blood. Alcohol is metabolized at a rate of $3/4$ ounce of absolute alcohol per hour. This is equal to one drink that contains $1\frac{1}{2}$ ounces of 100 proof hard liquor, 4 ounces of wine, or 8 ounces of beer. If a person drinks faster than this rate, the blood and brain alcohol levels rise and mood and behavior changes occur.

Women generally weigh less than men and also have a higher proportion of body fat to water. Thus, a woman achieves a higher level of alcohol in her blood faster than a man of the same size who drinks the same amount. The effect of alcohol also can vary with the stage of the menstrual cycle due to changes in the amount of body fluid. Just before menstruation, a woman retains fluid. There is more water in the body for the alcohol to be diluted in, thus the alcohol has less effect. In the middle of the menstrual cycle, when a woman is losing fluid, the same amount of alcohol can have a much stronger effect.

Those who are alcohol dependent have no ability to control their alcohol intake. Drinking takes place in response to intense internal mental and physical demands of which the drinker is often not aware. When this occurs, alcohol can disrupt relationships and pose serious health risks.

In addition to the personal misery and social distress suffered by a woman who abuses alcohol, her life span is about 15 years shorter than that of the average woman because of accidents that occur while drinking and as a result of damage to organs in the body. Not only does alcohol increase the risk of injuries from falls and driving accidents, it also makes a woman vulnerable to being the victim of robbery, physical abuse, and date rape. Alcohol abuse damages the heart, liver, ovaries, brain, nerves, muscles, and blood cells, and can lead to certain types of cancer. It causes damage directly by attacking the delicate membranes surrounding cells and indirectly because of the poor nutrition that usually goes along with heavy drinking. In addition to death from liver failure, hemorrhage, or severe brain damage, alcohol causes illnesses such as inflammation of the liver (hepatitis); inflammation of the pancreas; heart failure; damage to the bone marrow, causing anemia; and severe memory loss. Alcohol also has effects unique to women that result in risks to their health as well as that of their future children.

# ALCOHOL AND THE SPECIAL CONCERNS OF WOMEN

Most studies on alcohol and alcohol-related problems are based on men, and the results are different when these studies are repeated in women. Physically and mentally, women respond differently to alcohol than do men, and the impact of alcohol appears to be greater on women than men:

- *Depression.* People who abuse alcohol often feel depressed, and alcohol can increase depression. The incidence of suicide attempts is higher in alcoholic women than in the female population as a whole.

- *Liver damage.* Women are more susceptible to alcohol-related liver damage. They develop liver disease in a shorter time and at lower levels of consumption than do men. The number of alcoholic women who develop alcohol-related liver disease is higher than among alcoholic men.

- *Cancer.* Alcohol has been linked to cancer of the breast, although the relationship is unclear. There does seem to be an association between alcohol use and hormone levels, causing changes in a woman's menstrual function. With excess drinking, menstruation may become irregular or stop, and fertility is decreased.

- *Fetal damage.* Drinking during pregnancy can pose serious risks to the fetus. The more a woman drinks, the greater the danger, especially in the early stages of pregnancy. When a woman drinks, the alcohol quickly reaches the fetus through the placenta and can damage its delicate systems while they are being developed. Alcohol also increases the risk of miscarriage.

The most serious risk of drinking during pregnancy is *fetal alcohol syndrome.* This is the most common cause of mental retardation in babies. Babies are shorter, weigh less, have heart and facial defects, and have poor control over body movements. Children with fetal alcohol syndrome often are hyperactive; they are nervous, jittery, and have poor attention spans. It is not known how much alcohol can cause fetal alcohol syndrome, so it is recommended that pregnant women do not drink any alcohol.

## WHEN DRINKING BECOMES A PROBLEM

It is difficult to know how much alcohol is too much or when use becomes abuse. The effects vary with the individual and depend on a variety of factors such as what motivates her to drink, her patterns of drinking, and how often and how much she drinks. Certain tests can show signs of a drinking problem (see boxes on CAGE and T-ACE questionnaires). There are also some warning signs of a drinking problem:

- Having an auto accident after leaving a party in a state of intoxication
- Missing work or being late to work because of a hangover
- Not being able to perform housework or daily functions

- Having memory lapses or blackouts
- Having intercourse with someone to whom you would not ordinarily be attracted
- Fighting with friends or hitting one's children
- Being preoccupied with drinking and organizing activities and social functions around it
- Having marriage or family problems in which drinking could be a factor

Some drinking patterns may be a sign of trouble with alcohol:

- Being intoxicated more than once or twice a year
- Drinking more than a glass of wine or an occasional beer when alone
- Drinking to relieve stress or to allay anxiety
- Drinking to relieve insomnia, tension, depression, or pain
- Drinking after a party is over or the next morning to relieve a hangover

A person who has a problem with alcohol use may be reluctant to think about it or to seek advice for fear of being labeled an alcoholic. The label is not as important, however, as the effect on that person's life. Alcoholism is a disease that needs treatment. A woman who is drinking more than she would like to, who is having difficulty controlling her alcohol intake, or who finds that alcohol is having a disruptive effect on her life should seek help.

## Getting Help

More and more women are seeking professional help for alcoholism as they confront the incompatibility between the economic reality of gainful employment and the compelling need to drink. One in every three members of Alcoholics Anonymous (AA) is now a woman; many women attend employer-sponsored alcoholism treatment programs.

Alcoholics Anonymous has led the way in demonstrating the effectiveness of self-help. Meetings are held throughout the United States and Canada and the 2 million members are committed to the

---

### CAGE QUESTIONNAIRE

A positive response to even one of the first three questions may be an early sign of a drinking problem. A positive response to the last question is considered a sign of a more serious problem that requires treatment.

C    Have you ever felt you ought to CUT DOWN on your drinking?

A    Have people ANNOYED you by criticizing your drinking?

G    Have you ever felt bad or GUILTY about your drinking?

E    Have you ever had a drink first thing in the morning to steady your nerves or get rid of a hangover (EYE OPENER)?

*Source:* J. A. Ewing, Detecting Alcoholism: The CAGE Questionnaire. *Journal of the American Medical Association* 252 (1984): 1907.

common goal of maintaining their sobriety one day at a time.

Alcoholism is a family problem and can afflict any member. The alcoholic should be confronted with the problem and directed to help. In addition to Alcoholics Anonymous, other groups such as Al-Anon, Al-Ateen, and the National Association for Children of Alcoholics may be helpful (see box on Additional Resources).

---

## T–ACE QUESTIONNAIRE

For the TOLERANCE question, an answer of more than two drinks is considered a positive response. A score of 2 is assigned for a positive response to the TOLERANCE question, and a score of 1 is assigned to all others for positive responses. A T-ACE score of 2 or greater is considered a sign of a drinking problem.

T    How many drinks does it take to make you feel high (TOLERANCE)?
A    Have people ANNOYED you by criticizing your drinking?
C    Have you felt you ought to CUT DOWN on your drinking?
E    Have you ever had a drink first thing in the morning to steady your nerves or get rid of a hangover (EYE OPENER)?

*Source:* R. J. Sokol, S. S. Martier, J. W. Ager, "The T-ACE Questions: Practical Prenatal Detection of Risk-Drinking." *American Journal of Obstetrics and Gynecology* 160 (1989): 865.

---

Professional treatment is available through physicians and counselors such as psychiatrists, psychologists, and social workers. Their services may be available privately or through clinics, hospitals, or rehabilitation centers. Other sources of help include community mental health centers or programs available through employers. In major cities the National Council on Alcoholism has affiliates that maintain a list of treatment sources.

# PRESCRIPTION DRUGS

It is estimated that up to 2 percent of Americans use psychotherapeutic drugs—tranquilizers, sleeping pills, stimulants, and painkillers. Because of the mind-altering capability of these drugs, they have a potential for misuse. Misuse becomes abuse when these drugs are taken in greater amounts or for purposes other than those for which they were prescribed. Misuse can result in a psychological or physical dependency or both. Although these drugs can bring relief of symptoms such as anxiety, sleeplessness, and pain, they also have side effects and hazards that should be weighed against their benefits.

## Tranquilizers

Properly used, tranquilizers can provide short-term treatment of anxiety and stress caused by emotional conflict or a sudden trauma. They should be considered a bridge to other, more long-term forms of therapy and should always be used under the direction of a doctor.

The effect of tranquilizers on the brain is similar to that of alcohol. Low doses bring a feeling of relaxation and cheerfulness, while higher doses cause intoxication. Long-term use can lead to dependency similar to alcohol. When the drug is stopped symptoms such as severe anxiety, jitteriness, and insomnia can appear. Some women experience severe withdrawal symptoms, including emotional distress, dizziness, restlessness, headaches, and gastrointestinal upsets.

Women who are at risk of abusing drugs should not use tranquilizers. Signs of abuse include using more of the drug than prescribed, increasing the dose, or using tranquilizers to get intoxicated.

## Sleeping Pills

Drugs to relieve insomnia, known as hypnotics, include barbiturates and benzodiazepines. Although these drugs may have a value in certain short-term circumstances, long-term use can cause more harm than good. Prolonged use of sleeping pills can lead to dependency and side effects that continue after the person stops taking the drug. Tolerance can develop quickly and it becomes necessary to increase the amount of the drug to achieve the same effect. With increasing use, the effects of these drugs persist the next day and can result in mental cloudiness, poor concentration, memory difficulties, mood swings, anxiety, depression, and irritability. Withdrawal effects are similar to those of tranquilizers but may be more severe.

## Amphetamines

Stimulants such as benzedrine and dexedrine were once prescribed for weight loss. These drugs increase energy and depress appetite, which makes them appealing and, at the same time, subject to abuse. The body adapts quickly to these drugs, however, so after an initial weight loss, appetite returns and the weight is regained. For this reason, as well as because of their tendency to produce psychological and physical dependence, these drugs have been banned for weight-reduction purposes by the Food and Drug Administration. Often they are used illegally, however, to boost the effects of other drugs. Long-term use can result in agitation and insomnia, and they have a high potential for overdose.

## Painkillers

Addictive painkillers are related in some way to opium. Some are derivatives of morphine, whereas others share some of its properties. They include prescription pain-relief drugs as well as heroin and methadone. Painkillers have long-lasting effects, mainly on the brain, nervous system, and muscles, producing a sense of well-being, relaxation, and decreased sensitivity to pain. Side effects include constipation and kidney disease. Painkillers are highly addictive and, when withdrawn, cause physical and mental symptoms that can be serious.

# ILLICIT DRUGS

Illegal drug use is widespread and affects people of all backgrounds. According to a recent survey, 7 percent of Americans use illegal drugs, such as marijuana, cocaine, and opiates. Of the nearly 60 million women of childbearing age (15–44 years), over 5 million (9 percent) use marijuana or cocaine monthly if not more frequently. (See Figs. 4.2 and 4.3)

In addition to the effects of the drugs themselves, drug use poses other risks that relate to an unhealthy lifestyle. Female drug abusers have a higher incidence of sexually transmitted diseases, believed to stem from the practice of trading sex for drugs. Drug abusers also suffer from poor nutrition, making them susceptible to illness. Drug users who share needles are at risk of getting infections such as hepatitis B virus and human immunodeficiency virus, which causes acquired immune deficiency disease (AIDS).

Abuse of illicit drugs during pregnancy can pose serious problems for the fetus. Both cocaine and heroin can cause preterm birth and fetal death. When a woman uses drugs during pregnancy, her baby can become addicted to them just as she can. Babies born with an addiction show signs of withdrawal from the drug soon after birth.

## Cocaine

Derived from the coca plant, cocaine can be snorted, injected, or smoked. The availability of crack cocaine, a pure form of the drug that is smoked, has

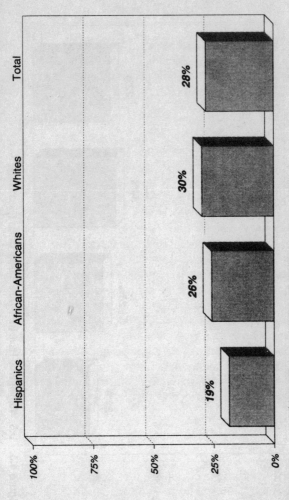

**Figure 4.2.** U.S. Women Who Have Used Marijuana (%, 1992).

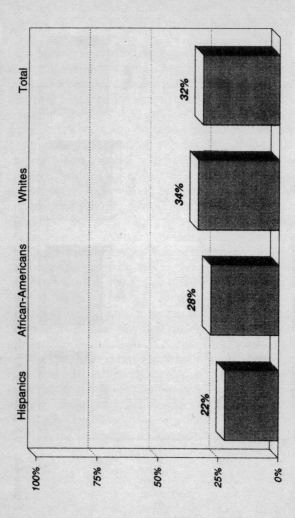

**Figure 4.3.** U.S. Women Who Have Used Other Illegal Drugs (%, 1992).

led to its widespread use. It is estimated that about 5 million men and women in the United States are regular users.

Shortly after it is ingested, cocaine produces an intense sense of euphoria and well-being that lasts about 30 minutes. Other effects include heightened self-confidence, a rush of energy, increased sensuality, and loss of appetite. The high is rapidly followed by a low, which increases the urge to repeat the drug and leads to addiction. Prolonged use results in nervousness, insomnia, inability to concentrate, fatigue, anxiety, and depression. The crack form of cocaine, because it is the quickest and most effective way to achieve the high, is the most popular form of the drug. It is also the most addictive, with addiction occurring within 6 months of use.

Regardless of how it is ingested cocaine affects all the major body systems. It causes an effect similar to a burst of adrenaline, increasing the heart rate, blood pressure, breathing rate, and temperature. This type of body stress places a great demand on the heart and blood vessels and can lead to chest pain, heart attack, or stroke. Cocaine also stimulates the brain and can cause seizures and convulsions. When used repeatedly, cocaine causes cells to die from lack of oxygen. When it is snorted, for instance, the dead cells in the nose become irritated and swell, causing congestion. Eventually, so many cells may die that a hole appears in the membrane separating the nostrils, which requires corrective surgery.

## Narcotics

Opiates, also known as narcotics, are drugs distilled from opium that dull the senses, relieve pain, and produce sleep. They are used as pain relievers (see Table 4.1) and abused as illegal drugs such as heroin. Heroin can be ingested by snorting or injection. The latter method produces prompt effects that last from 3 to 4 hours. Heroin addiction can develop quickly and serious health problems result with chronic use. An overdose can suppress the central nervous system to the point where the heart and lungs cease to function.

Withdrawal symptoms—sweating, tremors, cramps, anxiety, and an intense craving for the drug—occur soon after a person stops taking the drug. Methadone, a synthetic substitute for heroin, is sometimes given to heroin addicts to help them function without heroin. Information and referral for methadone programs and other types of treatment as well as support groups can be obtained through hospitals and social service groups in the community.

## Hallucinogens

Hallucinogens include substances derived from organic materials, such as marijuana and hashish, as well as synthetic agents such as LSD and PCP (angel dust). They all produce effects on the central nervous system that alter perception and body function. The effects are more long lasting with some forms of drugs than with others.

Marijuana and hashish produce a mood that is

calm, reflective, and detached. Hallucinations are rare with these substances, but they can occur, as can panic attacks. Marijuana is retained in the fatty tissues for several days before it is processed by the body, although there is no evidence that prolonged use causes permanent damage. Chronic heavy use may cause loss of energy and drive and result in psychological dependence, which is indicated by a preoccupation with the drug and an inability to control its use.

The hallucinogens PCP and LSD share many similar properties. They produce vivid changes in sensation and perception, conveying euphoria, or alteration in the sense of passage of time. Both agents are thought to worsen latent schizophrenia. Their use may lead to chronic psychosis, flashbacks, and violent behavior.

# INFORMED AVOIDANCE OF SUBSTANCE ABUSE

An increasing number of contemporary women are using psychoactive substances, ranging from nicotine and alcohol to tranquilizers, stimulants, and opiates. The reasons for this trend are varied and complicated but no doubt are connected to the pressures that today's society places on women to juggle the demands of job and family. Fortunately, women have access to information and resources to help them make informed decisions. Women can take control of their health and that of their families by being fully informed, active participants in decisions about drug use. This means awareness of certain key concepts:

- Nicotine can end a life before its time.
- Alcohol can cause a woman to lose control of her life and lead to major health problems.
- Drugs can cause physical and mental dependency.

---

## ADDITIONAL RESOURCES

American Cancer Society
  800-ACS-2345

American Heart Association
  800-AHA-8721

American Lung Association
  800-Lung-USA

National Heart, Lung, and Blood Institute
  301-251-1222

National Cancer Institute
  800-4-CANCER

Office on Smoking and Health
  Centers for Disease Control
  800-CDC-1311

American Society for Addiction Medicine
  301-656-3920

By being alert to warning signs and doing something about them, women can avoid the problems associated with drug use. Counseling and treatment are available at local and national levels; these programs are effective in helping women help themselves to lead healthier lives free of the mental and physical effects of drugs.

## EDITORS AND CONTRIBUTORS

### MEDICAL CO-EDITORS

ROSELYN PAYNE EPPS, M.D., M.P.H., M.A., F.A.A.P., is an expert at the National Institutes of Health, Bethesda, Maryland, and a Professor at Howard University College of Medicine, Washington, D.C. She is recognized nationally and internationally in areas of health policy and research, health promotion and disease prevention, and medical education and health service delivery. As a pioneer and leader in numerous professional and community organizations, she served, in 1991, as the first African American president of AMWA and the founding president of the AMWA Foundation.

SUSAN COBB STEWART, M.D., F.A.C.P., is an internist and gastroenterologist, and is presently Associate Medical Director at J. P. Morgan in New York, where she delivers general medical care, specialty consultations, and preventive services. She is Clinical Assistant Professor of Medicine at SUNY, Brooklyn. Since serving as President of AMWA in 1990, Dr. Stewart has continued to help AMWA shape and focus its mission in the area of women's health.

### CONTRIBUTORS

Marjorie Braude, M.D., is a psychiatrist in private practice in Los Angeles, California, She has chaired the Domestic Violence Subcommittee of AMWA, and she chairs the City of Los Angeles Domestic Violence Task Force.

Leah J. Dickstein, M.D., F.A.P.A., is a professor in the Department of Psychiatry and Behavioral Sciences and Associate Dean for Faculty and Student Advocacy at the University of Louisville School of Medicine. She is a past president of AMWA (1992) and has served as vice president of the American Psychiatric Association.

Anne Geller, M.D., a neurologist, is Chief of the Smithers Addiction, Treatment, and Training Center in New York. She is Senior Attending Physician in Medicine at St. Luke's/Roosevelt Hospital Center and Associate Professor of Clinical Medicine at Columbia College of Physicians and Surgeons. She was the 1993–1995 president of the American Society of Addiction Medicine.

Jeanne Spurlock, M.D., F.A.P.A., is a Clinical Professor of Psychiatry at George Washington and Howard universities. She has been in private practice in Washington, D.C., since 1974. She is a former Deputy Medical Director and Director of the Office of Minority/National Affairs of the American Psychiatric Association.

# INDEX

Acaraphobia, 14
Acquired immune deficiency syndrome (AIDS), 75–76, 98, 130
Acrophobia, 14
Addictive personality traits, 104
Addison's disease, 36
Adolescence
  depression in, 17
  suicide in, 24
Adrenal cortex, 50
Adrenal glands, 36, 51
*Against Our Will: Men, Women and Rape* (Brownmiller), 71
Aging, fear of, 2
Agoraphobia, 13, 14
Ailurophobia, 13
Alcohol, 5, 11–12, 37, 40, 90, 93, 98, 99, 102, 117–127
  effects of, 120–121
  help for problem with, 125–127
  pregnancy and, 122–123
  warning signs of problem with, 123–126
Alcoholics Anonymous (AA), 125–126
Alprazolam (Xanax), 10
American Cancer Society, 107, 136
American Heart Association, 136
American Lung Association, 136
American Psychiatric Association, 32, 77
American Society for Addiction Medicine, 136
Amitriptyline (Elavil), 20
Amphetamines, 20, 129
Anorexia nervosa, 43–44
Antidepressants, 10, 12, 13, 19–21
Antipsychotics, 33–34
Anxiety, 2, 5, 6
  generalized anxiety disorder (GAD), 9–11

Anxiety (Cont.)
  obsessive-compulsive
    disorder (OCD), 9,
    11–12
  panic disorder, 9,
    12–13
  phobias, 9, 13–14
  post-traumatic stress
    disorder (PTSD), 9,
    14–15
Anxiolytics, 10
Arthritis, 52
Asthma, 52
Atypical depression, 20
Autonomic nervous sys-
  tem, 49
Avoidant personality
  disorder, 27

Barbiturates, 128
Battery (*see* Domestic
  battery)
Behavioral therapy, 8,
  10, 12–14, 44
Behavior therapy, 43
Belonephobia, 13
Benzedrine, 129
Benzodiazepines, 10, 128
Benztropine mesylate
  (Cogentin), 34
Binge eating, 43
Biofeedback, 6
Bipolar disorder, 21–23

Blood sugar, 4
"Blues," 2, 16
Body image, 2
Borderline personality
  disorder, 27–28
Brain trauma, 35
Brain tumors, 35
Breast cancer, 122
Breathing, 59–60
Bronchitis, 108–110
Brownmiller, Susan, 70,
  71
Bulimia, 43–44
Buspirone (Buspar), 10

Caffeine, 4, 11, 37
CAGE Questionnaire,
  123, 125
Cancers, 42, 105, 109,
  110, 113, 122
Carbamazepine
  (Tegretol), 23
Carbon monoxide, 105,
  106, 108
Cardiovascular disease,
  108
Catatonic schizophrenia,
  33
Centers for Disease
  Control and
  Prevention, 68, 136
Cerebral infection, 35
Cervical cancer, 109

Childhood sexual abuse, 67–69, 83–86
Chlorpromazine (Thorazine), 34
Chores, 56–57
Chronic muscle tension, 10
Chronic obstructive pulmonary disease (COPD), 110–111
Cigarette smoking, 5, 98, 102–117
  during pregnancy, 111–112
  impact on women, 107–111
  ingredients in cigarettes, 105–107
  passive, 110
  quitting, 112–117
Claustrophobia, 14
Clonazepam (Klonopin), 10
Cocaine, 130, 132
Coffee, 4
Cognitive therapy, 8, 31
Concentration, 9
Constipation, 20, 34
Consultations, 7
Continuous amnesia, 26
Cortisol, 51–52
Crack cocaine, 130, 132
Cushing's syndrome, 36
Cyclothymia, 22

Date rape, 66, 72–73
Denial, 78, 86
Dependent personality disorder, 28
Depression, 2–4, 6, 10, 15
  alcohol and, 122
  bipolar disorder, 21–23
  following rape, 78
  hormonal, 19–21
  suicidal thoughts, 23–24
  symptoms of, 16–18
Dexedrine, 129
Diabetes, 36, 41, 42
Diarrhea, 10
Diazepam (Valium), 10
Diet, 4, 43
Disorganized schizophrenia, 33
Dissociative amnesia, 26
Dissociative fugue, 26
Dissociative identity disorder, 25, 86
Diuretics, abuse of, 44
Dizziness, 9, 12, 20
Domestic battery, 66–68, 87–95
Doom, sense of impending, 9, 12

Dopamine, 34
Drugs, 5
  illicit, 101, 130–135
  pregnancy and,
    98–99, 130
  prescription,
    100–101, 127–129
Dry mouth, 9, 20, 34
Dual diagnosis, 40
Dysthymia, 22

Eating disorders, 2, 41–44
Eczema, 31
Elderly
  caring for, 2
  depression in, 17–18,
    24
  suicide and, 24
Electroshock therapy
  (EST), 21, 33
Emotional abuse, 87
Emphysema, 108, 111
Endocrine disorders,
  35–36
Endocrine system, 49
Endorphins, 4, 107
Epilepsy, 35
Exercise, 3–4, 37, 61–62

Family (dyadic) therapy, 8
Fatigue, 2, 3, 17
Fetal alcohol syndrome,
  123

Fight or flight response,
  4, 13, 49, 59
Fluoxetine (Prozac), 20

Gender-based violence,
  66–96 (see also Rape)
  childhood sexual
    abuse, 67–69,
    83–86
  domestic battery,
    66–68, 87–95
  effects of, 69–70
General adaptation
  reflex, 49
Generalized amnesia, 26
Generalized anxiety dis-
  order (GAD), 9–11
Goals, 56
Grandiosity, 21
Graves' disease, 36
Group therapy, 8, 44

Hallucinations, 15, 32
Hallucinogens, 99–101,
  134–135
Haloperidol (Haldol),
  34
Hashish, 134–135
Headaches, 10
Heart attacks, 108, 113
Heroin, 134
Histrionic personality
  disorder, 28

Hopelessness, 17
Hormonal depression, 19–21
Hypertension, 42, 108
Hypnotics, 128
Hypoglycemia, 3
Hypothalamus, 49–51
Hysterectomy, 19

Illicit drugs, 101, 130–135
Immune system, 52
Impotence, 20
Incest, 84, 86
Insomnia, 9, 10, 15, 17, 37–39
Intestinal problems, 9
Introversion, 22
Irritability, 9, 15, 19, 21
Isolation, 17, 30, 89

Laxatives, abuse of, 44
Leisure time, 6, 55–56
Lesbians, 40
Light therapy, 18
Limbic system, 49
Lithium, 20, 23
Liver damage, 122
Localized amnesia, 26
Locus coeruleus, 4, 13
LSD, 134, 135
Lung cancer, 105, 109, 110, 113

Mammary glands, 50
Manic-depressive disorder (*see* Bipolar disorder)
Marijuana, 130, 131, 134–135
Marriage therapy, 8
Meditation, 6
Medulla oblongata, 4
Melatonin, 18
Memory loss, 20, 21
Menopause, 2, 111
Menstruation, 120–122
Mental health specialists, 7
Methadone, 134
Migraine, 31
Monoamine oxidase (MAO) inhibitors, 20–21
Monophobia, 14
Morphine, 129
Multiple personality disorder (*see* Dissociative identity disorder)

Napping, 37
Narcissistic personality disorder, 29
Narcotics, 99–101, 134
National Association for Children of Alcoholics, 126

National Cancer Institute, 136
National Child Abuse Hotline, 85
National Clearinghouse for the Defense of Battered Women, 95
National Coalition Against Domestic Violence, 94
National Committee for Prevention of Child Abuse, 85
National Council on Alcoholism, 127
National Crime Victim Center, 67, 70
National Heart, Lung, and Blood Institute, 136
National Organization for Victims Assistance, 82
Neurotransmitters, 99
Nicotine, 105, 107, 108, 114, 115
Nightmares, 15
Norepinephrine, 13

Obesity, 41–42
Obsessive-compulsive disorder (OCD), 9, 11–12
Obsessive-compulsive personality disorder, 29

Ocholophobia, 14
Operant conditioning, 8
Opiates, 130, 134
Oral cavity diseases, 109
Osteoporosis, 111

Painkillers, 129
Palpitations, 9, 10, 12
Panic attacks, 3, 47
Panic disorder, 9, 12–13
Paranoid personality disorder, 29
Paranoid schizophrenia, 33
Parents Anonymous, 85
Paroxetine (Paxil), 20
Passive-aggressive personality disorder, 30
Passive smoking, 110
PCP (angel dust), 134, 135
Personality disorders, 27–32
Pessimism, 16
Phobias, 9, 13–14
Physical check-up, 3
Pineal gland, 18
Pituitary gland, 49, 50
Pneumonia, 109
Polypharmacy, 24
Postpartum depression, 19
Post-traumatic stress disorder (PTSD), 9, 14–15, 69, 77

Pregnancy
    abuse in, 91, 93
    alcohol use in,
        122–123
    depression in, 19
    drug use in, 98–99,
        130
    following rape, 76
    sleep in, 38
    smoking in, 111–112
Premenstrual dysphoric
    disorder (PMDD), 19
Premenstrual syndrome
    (PMS), 4, 5, 19
Prescription drugs,
    100–101, 127–129
Progressive relaxation,
    60–61
Psychiatric social
    workers, 7
Psychiatrists, 7
Psychoanalysis, 8, 10
Psychologists, 7
Psychotherapy, 7, 8, 27,
    44
Pterygophobia, 14

Rape, 15, 66, 67, 70–83
    aftermath of, 74–76,
        82
    date rape, 66, 72–73
    legal system and,
        79–80

    preventing, 73–74,
        80–81
    wartime, 70–71
Rape trauma syndrome,
    77–79
Rap music, 66, 88
Relaxation, 6, 13, 60–61
Restless leg syndrome,
    40–41

Sandwich generation, 2
Schizoid personality
    disorder, 30
Schizophrenia, 32–34
Schizotypal personality
    disorder, 30
Seasonal affective
    disorder (SAD), 18
Sedatives, 99–101
Selective amnesia, 26
Selective serotonin reup-
    take inhibitors, 13, 20
Self-esteem, 17, 27, 28,
    76, 78
Self-help groups, 6, 44
Senile dementia, 24
Sertraline (Zoloft), 20
Sexual abuse, 25, 66–69,
    83–86
Sexually transmitted dis-
    eases, 75, 130
Sinusitis, 108
Sitophobia, 14

Sleep apnea, 39
Sleep clinics, 42
Sleep disorders, 36–41
Sleeping pills, 100, 128
Sleep patterns, 4, 16–17, 38
Smoking (see Cigarette smoking)
Social life, 6
Somatoform disorders, 31
Stalking, 66, 68
Stimulants, 99–101, 129
Stress, 46–63
  behavioral change and, 55–59
  breathing, relaxation and exercise, 59–63
  hypothalamus and, 49–51
  physical symptoms of, 54
  psychological signs of, 53
  vulnerability of women, 52–55
Stroke, 35, 42
Substance abuse (see Alcohol; Cigarette smoking; Drugs)
Sugar, 4–5
Suicidal thoughts, 17, 23–24, 122
Sweating, 10, 12

Systematic desensitization, 14

T-ACE Questionnaire, 123, 126
Tardive dyskinesia, 34
Therapies, types of, 8–9
Thyroid gland, 3, 35–36, 50
Tobacco (see Cigarette smoking)
Tranquilizers, 33, 98, 100, 127–128
Tricyclic antidepressants, 13, 20
Triglycerides, 4

Urinary tract problems, 20, 52

Valproate (Depakote), 23
Violence Against Women Act Task Force, 83
Violence (see Gender-based violence)

Wartime rape, 70–71
War veterans, 15
Winter blues, 16, 18
Work, 5, 6

Yoga, 6
Yo-yo syndrome, 43